EPIC OF GILGAMESH

MORRIS JASTROW

ISBN: 1516986458
ISBN-13: 978-1516986453

EPIC OF GILGAMESH

An Old Babylonian Version of the Gilgamesh Epic

On the Basis of Recently Discovered Texts

By Morris Jastrow

&

Albert T. Clay

Gilgamesh is the oldest work of literature. When we look for the beginning of mankind the path before us is silent, raw materials that are in the residential and cage culture , heritage and sank into silence, keeping a lot of time in five thousands years back to back. Gilgamesh is the oldest record of human thought. The time , which has been limited to the possibility of the appearance of the spread . But the invention of Gutenberg extended the cultural revolution.

EPIC OF GILGAMESH

Introduction

The Gilgamesh Epic is the most notable literary product of Babylonia as yet discovered in the mounds of Mesopotamia. It recounts the exploits and adventures of a favorite hero, and in its final form covers twelve tablets, each tablet consisting of six columns (three on the obverse and three on the reverse) of about 50 lines for each column, or a total of about 3600 lines. Of this total, however, barely more than one-half has been found among the remains of the great collection of cuneiform tablets gathered by King Ashurbanapal (668–626 B.C.) in his palace at Nineveh, and discovered by Layard in 18541 in the course of his excavations of the mound Kouyunjik (opposite Mosul). The fragments of the epic painfully gathered—chiefly by George Smith—from the *circa* 30,000 tablets and bits of tablets brought to the British Museum were published in model form by Professor Paul Haupt;2 and that edition still remains the primary source for our study of the Epic.

For the sake of convenience we may call the form of the Epic in the fragments from the library of Ashurbanapal the Assyrian version, though like most of the literary productions in the library it not only reverts to a Babylonian original, but represents a late copy of a much older original. The absence of any reference to Assyria in the fragments recovered justifies us in assuming that the Assyrian version received its present form in Babylonia, perhaps in Erech; though it is of course possible that some of the late features, particularly the elaboration of the teachings of the theologians or schoolmen in the eleventh and twelfth tablets, may have been produced at least in part under Assyrian influence. A definite indication that the Gilgamesh Epic reverts to a period earlier than Hammurabi (or Hammurawi)3 i.e., beyond 2000 B. C., was furnished by the publication of a text clearly belonging to the first Babylonian dynasty (of which Hammurabi was the sixth member) in *CT.* VI, 5; which text Zimmern4 recognized as a part of the tale of Atra-ḫasis, one of the names given to the survivor of the deluge, recounted on the eleventh tablet of the Gilgamesh Epic.5 This was confirmed by the discovery6 of a fragment of the deluge story dated in the eleventh year of Ammisaduka, i.e., c. 1967 B.C. In this text, likewise, the name of the deluge hero appears as Atra-ḫasis (col. VIII, 4).7 But while these two tablets do not belong to the Gilgamesh Epic and merely introduce an episode which has also been incorporated into the Epic, Dr. Bruno Meissner in 1902 published a tablet, dating, as the writing and the internal evidence showed, from the Hammurabi period, which undoubtedly is a portion of what by way of distinction we may call an old Babylonian version.8 It was picked up by Dr. Meissner at a dealer's shop in Bagdad and acquired for the Berlin Museum. The tablet consists of four columns (two on the obverse and two on the reverse) and deals with the hero's wanderings in search of a cure from disease with which he has been smitten after the death of his companion Enkidu. The hero fears that the disease will be fatal and longs to escape death. It corresponds to a portion of Tablet X of the Assyrian version. Unfortunately, only the lower portion of the obverse and the upper of the reverse have been preserved (57 lines in all); and in default of a colophon we do not know the numeration of the tablet in this old Babylonian edition. Its chief value, apart from its furnishing a proof for the existence of the Epic as early as 2000 B. C., lies (a) in the writing *Gish* instead of Gish-gi(n)-mash in the Assyrian version, for the name of the hero, (b) in the writing En-ki-dũ—abbreviated from dũg— "Enki is good" for En-ki-dú in the Assyrian version,9 and (c) in the remarkable address of the maiden Sabitum, dwelling at the seaside, to whom Gilgamesh comes in the course of his wanderings. From the Assyrian version we know that the hero tells the maiden of his grief for his lost companion, and of his longing to escape the dire fate of Enkidu. In the old Babylonian fragment the answer of Sabitum is given in full, and the sad note that it strikes, showing how hopeless it is for man to try to escape death which is in store for all mankind, is as remarkable as is the philosophy of "eat, drink and be merry" which Sabitum imparts. The address indicates how early the tendency arose to attach to ancient tales the current religious teachings.

"Why, O Gish, does thou run about?

The life that thou seekest, thou wilt not find.

When the gods created mankind,

Death they imposed on mankind;

Life they kept in their power.

Thou, O Gish, fill thy belly,

Day and night do thou rejoice,

Daily make a rejoicing!

Day and night a renewal of jollification!

Let thy clothes be clean,

Wash thy head and pour water over thee!

Care for the little one who takes hold of thy hand!

Let the wife rejoice in thy bosom!"

Such teachings, reminding us of the leading thought in the Biblical Book of Ecclesiastes,10 indicate the *didactic* character given to ancient tales that were of popular origin, but which were modified and elaborated under the influence of the schools which arose in connection with the Babylonian temples. The story itself belongs, therefore, to a still earlier period than the form it received in this old Babylonian version. The existence of this tendency at so early a date comes to us as a genuine surprise, and justifies the assumption that the attachment of a lesson to the deluge story in the Assyrian version, to wit, the limitation in attainment of immortality to those singled out by the gods as exceptions, dates likewise from the old Babylonian period. The same would apply to the twelfth tablet, which is almost entirely didactic, intended to illustrate the impossibility of learning anything of the fate of those who have passed out of this world. It also emphasizes the necessity of contenting oneself with the comfort that the care of the dead, by providing burial and food and drink offerings for them affords, as the only means of ensuring for them rest and freedom from the pangs of hunger and distress. However, it is of course possible that the twelfth tablet, which impresses one as a supplement to the adventures of Gilgamesh, ending with his return to Uruk (i.e., Erech) at the close of the eleventh tablet, may represent a *later* elaboration of the tendency to connect religious teachings with the exploits of a favorite hero.

We now have further evidence both of the extreme antiquity of the literary form of the Gilgamesh Epic and also of the disposition to make the Epic the medium of illustrating aspects of life and the destiny of mankind. The discovery by Dr. Arno Poebel of a Sumerian form of the tale of the descent of Ishtar to the lower world and her release11—apparently a nature myth to illustrate the change of season from summer to winter and back again to spring—enables us to pass beyond the Akkadian (or Semitic) form of tales current in the Euphrates Valley to the Sumerian form. Furthermore, we are indebted to Dr. Langdon for the identification of two Sumerian fragments in the Nippur Collection which deal with the adventures of Gilgamesh, one in Constantinople,[12] the other in the collection of the University of Pennsylvania Museum.[13] The former, of which only 25 lines are preserved (19 on the obverse and 6 on the reverse), appears to be a description of the weapons of Gilgamesh with which he arms himself for an encounter—presumably the encounter with Ḫumbaba or Ḫuwawa, the ruler of the cedar forest in the mountain.[14] The latter deals with the building operations of Gilgamesh in the city of Erech. A text in Zimmern's *Sumerische Kultlieder aus altbabylonischer Zeit* (Leipzig, 1913), No. 196, appears likewise to be a fragment of the Sumerian version of the Gilgamesh Epic, bearing on the episode of Gilgamesh's and Enkidu's relations to the goddess Ishtar, covered in the sixth and seventh tablets of the Assyrian version.[15]

Until, however, further fragments shall have turned up, it would be hazardous to institute a comparison between the Sumerian and the Akkadian versions. All that can be said for the present is that there is every reason to believe in the existence of a literary form of the Epic in Sumerian which presumably antedated the Akkadian recension, just as we have a Sumerian form of Ishtar's descent into the nether world, and Sumerian versions of creation myths, as also of the Deluge tale.[16] It does not follow, however, that the Akkadian versions of the Gilgamesh Epic are translations of the Sumerian, any more than that the Akkadian creation myths are translations of a Sumerian original. Indeed, in the case of the creation myths, the striking difference between the Sumerian and Akkadian views of creation[17] points to the independent production of creation stories on the part of the Semitic settlers of the Euphrates Valley, though no doubt these were worked out in part under Sumerian literary influences. The same is probably true of Deluge tales, which would be given a distinctly Akkadian coloring in being reproduced and steadily elaborated by the Babylonian *literati* attached to the temples. The presumption is, therefore, in favor of an independent *literary* origin for the Semitic versions of the Gilgamesh Epic, though naturally with a duplication of the episodes, or at least of some of them, in the Sumerian narrative. Nor does the existence of a Sumerian form of the Epic necessarily prove that it originated with the

Sumerians in their earliest home before they came to the Euphrates Valley. They may have adopted it after their conquest of southern Babylonia from the Semites who, there are now substantial grounds for believing, were the earlier settlers in the Euphrates Valley.18 We must distinguish, therefore, between the earliest *literary* form, which was undoubtedly Sumerian, and the *origin* of the episodes embodied in the Epic, including the chief actors, Gilgamesh and his companion Enkidu. It will be shown that one of the chief episodes, the encounter of the two heroes with a powerful guardian or ruler of a cedar forest, points to a western region, more specifically to Amurru, as the scene. The names of the two chief actors, moreover, appear to have been "Sumerianized" by an artificial process,19 and if this view turns out to be correct, we would have a further ground for assuming the tale to have originated among the Akkadian settlers and to have been taken over from them by the Sumerians.

New light on the earliest Babylonian version of the Epic, as well as on the Assyrian version, has been shed by the recovery of two substantial fragments of the form which the Epic had assumed in Babylonia in the Hammurabi period. The study of this important new material also enables us to advance the interpretation of the Epic and to perfect the analysis into its component parts. In the spring of 1914, the Museum of the University of Pennsylvania acquired by purchase a large tablet, the writing of which as well as the style and the manner of spelling verbal forms and substantives pointed distinctly to the time of the first Babylonian dynasty. The tablet was identified by Dr. Arno Poebel as part of the Gilgamesh Epic; and, as the colophon showed, it formed the second tablet of the series. He copied it with a view to publication, but the outbreak of the war which found him in Germany—his native country—prevented him from carrying out this intention.20 He, however, utilized some of its contents in his discussion of the historical or semi-historical traditions about Gilgamesh, as revealed by the important list of partly mythical and partly historical dynasties, found among the tablets of the Nippur collection, in which Gilgamesh occurs21 as a King of an Erech dynasty, whose father was Â, a priest of Kulab.22

The publication of the tablet was then undertaken by Dr. Stephen Langdon in monograph form under the title, "The Epic of Gilgamish."23 In a preliminary article on the tablet in the *Museum Journal*, Vol. VIII, pages 29–38, Dr. Langdon took the tablet to be of the late Persian period (i.e., between the sixth and third century B. C.), but his attention having been called to this error of some *1500 years*, he corrected it in his introduction to his edition of the text, though he neglected to change some of his notes in which he still refers to the text as "late."24 In addition to a copy of the text, accompanied by a good photograph, Dr. Langdon furnished a transliteration and translation with some notes and a brief introduction. The text is unfortunately badly copied, being full of errors; and the translation is likewise very defective. A careful collation with the original tablet was made with the assistance of Dr. Edward Chiera, and as a consequence we are in a position to offer to scholars a correct text. We beg to acknowledge our obligations to Dr. Gordon, the Director of the Museum of the University of Pennsylvania, for kindly placing the tablet at our disposal. Instead of republishing the text, I content myself with giving a full list of corrections in the appendix to this volume which will enable scholars to control our readings, and which will, I believe, justify the translation in the numerous passages in which it deviates from Dr. Langdon's rendering. While credit should be given to Dr. Langdon for having made this important tablet accessible, the interests of science demand that attention be called to his failure to grasp the many important data furnished by the tablet, which escaped him because of his erroneous readings and faulty translations.

The tablet, consisting of six columns (three on the obverse and three on the reverse), comprised, according to the colophon, 240 lines25 and formed the second tablet of the series. Of the total, 204 lines are preserved in full or in part, and of the missing thirty-six quite a number can be restored, so that we have a fairly complete tablet. The most serious break occurs at the top of the reverse, where about eight lines are missing. In consequence of this the connection between the end of the obverse (where about five lines are missing) and the beginning of the reverse is obscured, though not to the extent of our entirely losing the thread of the narrative.

About the same time that the University of Pennsylvania Museum purchased this second tablet of the Gilgamesh Series, Yale University obtained a tablet from the same dealer, which turned out to be a continuation of the University of Pennsylvania tablet. That the two belong to the same edition of the Epic is shown by their agreement in the dark brown color of the clay, in the writing as well as in the size of the tablet, though the characters on the Yale tablet are somewhat cramped and in consequence more difficult to read. Both tablets consist of six columns, three on the obverse and three on the reverse. The measurements of both are about the same, the Pennsylvania tablet being estimated at about 7 inches high, as against 72/16 inches for the Yale tablet, while the width of both is 6½ inches. The Yale tablet is, however, more closely written and therefore has a larger number of lines than the Pennsylvania tablet. The colophon to the Yale tablet is unfortunately missing, but from internal evidence it is quite certain that the Yale tablet follows immediately upon the Pennsylvania tablet and, therefore, may be set down as the third of the series. The obverse is very badly preserved, so that only a general view of its contents can be secured. The reverse contains serious gaps in the first and second columns. The scribe evidently had a copy before him which he tried to follow exactly, but finding that he could not get all of the copy before him in the six columns, he continued the last column on the edge. In this way we obtain for the sixth column 64 lines as against 45 for column IV, and 47 for column V, and a total of 292 lines for the six columns. Subtracting the 16 lines written on the edge leaves us 276 lines for our tablet as against 240 for its companion. The width of each column being the same on both tablets, the difference of 36 lines is made up by the closer writing.

Both tablets have peculiar knobs at the sides, the purpose of which is evidently not to facilitate holding the tablet in one's hand while writing or reading it, as Langdon assumed26 (it would be quite impracticable for this purpose), but simply to protect the tablet in its position on a shelf, where it would naturally be placed on the edge, just as we arrange books on a shelf. Finally be it noted that these two tablets of the old Babylonian version do not belong to the same edition as the Meissner tablet above described, for the latter consists of two columns each on obverse and reverse, as against three columns each in the case of our two tablets. We thus have the interesting proof that as early as 2000 B.C. there were already several editions of the Epic. As to the provenance of our two tablets, there are no definite data, but it is likely that they were found by natives in the mounds at Warka, from which about the year 1913, many tablets came into the hands of dealers. It is likely that where two tablets of a series were found, others of the series were also dug up, and we may expect to find some further portions of this old Babylonian version turning up in the hands of other dealers or in museums.

Coming to the contents of the two tablets, the Pennsylvania tablet deals with the meeting of the two heroes, Gilgamesh and Enkidu, their conflict, followed by their reconciliation, while the Yale tablet in continuation takes up the preparations for the encounter of the two heroes with the guardian of the cedar forest, Ḫumbaba—but probably pronounced Ḫubaba[27]—or, as the name appears in the old Babylonian version, Ḫuwawa. The two tablets correspond, therefore, to portions of Tablets I to V of the Assyrian version;[28] but, as will be shown in detail further on, the number of *completely* parallel passages is not large, and the Assyrian version shows an independence of the old Babylonian version that is larger than we had reason to expect. In general, it may be said that the Assyrian version is more elaborate, which points to its having received its present form at a considerably later period than the old Babylonian version.[29] On the other hand, we already find in the Babylonian version the tendency towards repetition, which is characteristic of Babylonian-Assyrian tales in general. Through the two Babylonian tablets we are enabled to fill out certain details of the two episodes with which they deal: (1) the meeting of Gilgamesh and Enkidu, and (2) the encounter with Ḫuwawa; while their greatest value consists in the light that they throw on the gradual growth of the Epic until it reached its definite form in the text represented by the fragments in Ashurbanapal's Library. Let us now take up the detailed analysis, first of the Pennsylvania tablet and then of the Yale tablet. The Pennsylvania tablet begins with two dreams recounted by Gilgamesh to his mother, which the latter interprets as presaging the coming of Enkidu to Erech. In the one, something like a heavy meteor falls from heaven upon Gilgamesh and almost crushes him. With the help of the heroes of Erech, Gilgamesh carries the heavy burden to his mother Ninsun. The burden, his mother explains, symbolizes some one who, like Gilgamesh, is born in the mountains, to whom all will pay homage and of whom Gilgamesh will become enamoured with a love as strong as that for a woman. In a second dream, Gilgamesh sees some one who is like him, who brandishes an axe, and with whom he falls in love. This personage, the mother explains, is again Enkidu.

Langdon is of the opinion that these dreams are recounted to Enkidu by a woman with whom Enkidu cohabits for six days and seven nights and who weans Enkidu from association with animals. This, however, cannot be correct. The scene between Enkidu and the woman must have been recounted in detail in the first tablet, as in the Assyrian version,30 whereas here in the second tablet we have the continuation of the tale with Gilgamesh recounting his dreams directly to his mother. The story then continues with the description of the coming of Enkidu, conducted by the woman to the outskirts of Erech, where food is given him. The main feature of the incident is the conversion of Enkidu to civilized life. Enkidu, who hitherto had gone about naked, is clothed by the woman. Instead of sucking milk and drinking from a trough like an animal, food and strong drink are placed before him, and he is taught how to eat and drink in human fashion. In human fashion he also becomes drunk, and his "spree" is naïvely described: "His heart became glad and his face shone."31 Like an animal, Enkidu's body had hitherto been covered with hair, which is now shaved off. He is anointed with oil, and clothed "like a man." Enkidu becomes a shepherd, protecting the fold against wild beasts, and his exploit in dispatching lions is briefly told. At this point—the end of column 3 (on the obverse), i.e., line 117, and the beginning of column 4 (on the reverse), i.e., line 131—a gap of 13 lines—the tablet is obscure, but apparently the story of Enkidu's gradual transformation from savagery to civilized life is continued, with stress upon his introduction to domestic ways with the wife chosen or decreed for him, and with work as part of his fate. All this has no connection with Gilgamesh, and it is evident that the tale of Enkidu was originally an *independent* tale to illustrate the evolution of man's career and destiny, how through intercourse with a woman he awakens to the sense of human dignity, how he becomes accustomed to the ways of civilization, how he passes through the pastoral stage to higher walks of life, how the family is instituted, and how men come to be engaged in the labors associated with human activities. In order to connect this tale with the Gilgamesh story, the two heroes are brought together; the woman taking on herself, in addition to the rôle of civilizer, that of the medium through which Enkidu is brought to Gilgamesh. The woman leads Enkidu from the outskirts of Erech into the city itself, where the people on seeing him remark upon his likeness to Gilgamesh. He is the very counterpart of the latter, though somewhat smaller in stature. There follows the encounter between the two heroes in the streets of Erech, where they engage in a fierce combat. Gilgamesh is overcome by Enkidu and is enraged at being thrown to the ground. The tablet closes with the endeavor of Enkidu to pacify Gilgamesh. Enkidu declares that the mother of Gilgamesh has exalted her son above the ordinary mortal, and that Enlil himself has singled him out for royal prerogatives.

After this, we may assume, the two heroes become friends and together proceed to carry out certain exploits, the first of which is an attack upon the mighty guardian of the cedar forest. This is the main episode in the Yale tablet, which, therefore, forms the third tablet of the old Babylonian version.

In the first column of the obverse of the Yale tablet, which is badly preserved, it would appear that the elders of Erech (or perhaps the people) are endeavoring to dissuade Gilgamesh from making the attempt to penetrate to the abode of Ḫuwawa. If this is correct, then the close of the first column may represent a conversation between these elders and the woman who accompanies Enkidu. It would be the elders who are represented as "reporting the speech to the woman," which is presumably the determination of Gilgamesh to fight Ḫuwawa. The elders apparently desire Enkidu to accompany Gilgamesh in this perilous adventure, and with this in view appeal to the woman. In the second column after an obscure reference to the mother of Gilgamesh—perhaps appealing to the sun-god—we find Gilgamesh and Enkidu again face to face. From the reference to Enkidu's eyes "filled with tears," we may conclude that he is moved to pity at the thought of what will happen to Gilgamesh if he insists upon carrying out his purpose. Enkidu, also, tries to dissuade Gilgamesh. This appears to be the main purport of the dialogue between the two, which begins about the middle of the second column and extends to the end of the third column. Enkidu pleads that even his strength is insufficient,

"My arms are lame,

My strength has become weak." (lines 88–89)

Gilgamesh apparently asks for a description of the terrible tyrant who thus arouses the fear of Enkidu, and in reply Enkidu tells him how at one time, when he was roaming about with the cattle, he penetrated into the forest and heard the roar of Ḫuwawa which was like that of a deluge. The mouth of the tyrant emitted fire, and his breath was death. It is clear, as Professor Haupt has suggested,32 that Enkidu furnishes the description of a volcano in eruption, with its mighty roar, spitting forth fire and belching out a suffocating smoke. Gilgamesh is, however, undaunted and urges Enkidu to accompany him in the adventure.

"I will go down to the forest," says Gilgamesh, if the conjectural restoration of the line in question (l. 126) is correct. Enkidu replies by again drawing a lurid picture of what will happen "When we go (together) to the forest……." This speech of Enkidu is continued on the reverse. In reply Gilgamesh emphasizes his reliance upon the good will of Shamash and reproaches Enkidu with cowardice. He declares himself superior to Enkidu's warning, and in bold terms says that he prefers to perish in the attempt to overcome Ḫuwawa rather than abandon it.

"Wherever terror is to be faced,

Thou, forsooth, art in fear of death.

Thy prowess lacks strength.

I will go before thee,

Though thy mouth shouts to me: 'thou art afraid to approach,'

If I fall, I will establish my name." (lines 143–148)

There follows an interesting description of the forging of the weapons for the two heroes in preparation for the encounter.[33] The elders of Erech when they see these preparations are stricken with fear. They learn of Ḫuwawa's threat to annihilate Gilgamesh if he dares to enter the cedar forest, and once more try to dissuade Gilgamesh from the undertaking.

"Thou art young, O Gish, and thy heart carries thee away,

Thou dost not know what thou proposest to do." (lines 190–191)

They try to frighten Gilgamesh by repeating the description of the terrible Ḫuwawa. Gilgamesh is still undaunted and prays to his patron deity Shamash, who apparently accords him a favorable "oracle" (*têrtu*). The two heroes arm themselves for the fray, and the elders of Erech, now reconciled to the perilous undertaking, counsel Gilgamesh to take provision along for the undertaking. They urge Gilgamesh to allow Enkidu to take the lead, for

"He is acquainted with the way, he has trodden the road

[to] the entrance of the forest." (lines 252–253)

The elders dismiss Gilgamesh with fervent wishes that Enkidu may track out the "closed path" for Gilgamesh, and commit him to the care of Lugalbanda—here perhaps an epithet of Shamash. They advise Gilgamesh to perform certain rites, to wash his feet in the stream of Ḫuwawa and to pour out a libation of water to Shamash. Enkidu follows in a speech likewise intended to encourage the hero; and with the actual beginning of the expedition against Ḫuwawa the tablet ends. The encounter itself, with the triumph of the two heroes, must have been described in the fourth tablet.

Now before taking up the significance of the additions to our knowledge of the Epic gained through these two tablets, it will be well to discuss the forms in which the names of the two heroes and of the ruler of the cedar forest occur in our tablets.

As in the Meissner fragment, the chief hero is invariably designated as ^{d}Gish in both the Pennsylvania and Yale tablets; and we may therefore conclude that this was the common form in the Hammurabi period, as against the writing ^{d}Gish-gì(n)-mash34 in the Assyrian version. Similarly, as in the Meissner fragment, the second hero's name is always written En-ki-dũ35 (abbreviated from dúg) as against En-ki-dú in the Assyrian version. Finally, we encounter in the Yale tablet for the first time the writing Ḫu-wa-wa as the name of the guardian of the cedar forest, as against Ḫum-ba-ba in the Assyrian version, though in the latter case, as we may now conclude from the Yale tablet, the name should rather be read Ḫu-ba-ba.36 The variation in the writing of the latter name is interesting as pointing to the aspirate pronunciation of the labial in both instances. The name would thus present a complete parallel to the Hebrew name Ḫowawa (or Ḫobab) who appears as the brother-in-law of Moses in the P document, Numbers 10, 29.37 Since the name also occurs, written precisely as in the Yale tablet, among the "Amoritic" names in the important lists published by Dr. Chiera,38 there can be no doubt that Ḫuwawa or Ḫubaba is a West Semitic name. This important fact adds to the probability that the "cedar forest" in which Ḫuwawa dwells is none other than the Lebanon district, famed since early antiquity for its cedars. This explanation of the name Ḫuwawa disposes of suppositions hitherto brought forward for an Elamitic origin. Gressmann39 still favors such an origin, though realizing that the description of the cedar forest points to the Amanus or Lebanon range. In further confirmation of the West Semitic origin of the name, we have in Lucian, *De Dea Syria*, § 19, the name Kombabos40 (the guardian of Stratonika), which forms a perfect parallel to Ḫu(m)baba. Of the important bearings of this western character of the name Ḫuwawa on the interpretation and origin of the Gilgamesh Epic, suggesting that the episode of the encounter between the tyrant and the two heroes rests upon a tradition of an expedition against the West or Amurru land, we shall have more to say further on.

The variation in the writing of the name Enkidu is likewise interesting. It is evident that the form in the old Babylonian version with the sign dū (i.e., dúg) is the original, for it furnishes us with a suitable etymology "Enki is good." The writing with dúg, pronounced dū, also shows that the sign dú as the third element in the form which the name has in the Assyrian version is to be read dú, and that former readings like Ea-bani must be definitely abandoned.41 The form with dú is clearly a *phonetic* writing of the Sumerian name, the sign dú being chosen to indicate the *pronunciation* (not the ideograph) of the third element dúg. This is confirmed by the writing En-gi-dú in the syllabary *CT* XVIII, 30, 10. The phonetic writing is, therefore, a warning against any endeavor to read the name by an Akkadian transliteration of the signs. This would not of itself prove that Enkidu is of Sumerian *origin*, for it might well be that the writing En-ki-dú is an endeavor to give a Sumerian *aspect* to a name that *may* have been foreign. The element dúg corresponds to the Semitic *ṭâbu*, "good," and En-ki being originally a designation of a deity as the "lord of the land," which would be the Sumerian manner of indicating a Semitic Baal, it is not at all impossible that En-ki-dúg may be the "Sumerianized" form of a Semitic בַּעַל טוֹב "Baal is good." It will be recalled that in the third column of the Yale tablet, Enkidu speaks of himself in his earlier period while still living with cattle, as wandering into the cedar forest of Ḫuwawa, while in another passage (ll. 252–253) he is described as "acquainted with the way ... to the entrance of the forest." This would clearly point to the West as the original home of Enkidu. We are thus led once more to Amurru—taken as a general designation of the West—as playing an important role in the Gilgamesh Epic.42 If Gilgamesh's expedition against Ḫuwawa of the Lebanon district recalls a Babylonian campaign against Amurru,

Enkidu's coming from his home, where, as we read repeatedly in the Assyrian version,

"He ate herbs with the gazelles,

Drank out of a trough with cattle,"43

may rest on a tradition of an Amorite invasion of Babylonia. The fight between Gilgamesh and Enkidu would fit in with this tradition, while the subsequent reconciliation would be the form in which the tradition would represent the enforced union between the invaders and the older settlers.

Leaving this aside for the present, let us proceed to a consideration of the relationship of the form ^{d}Gish, for the chief personage in the Epic in the old Babylonian version, to ^{d}Gish-gi(n)-mash in the Assyrian version. Of the meaning of Gish there is fortunately no doubt. It is clearly the equivalent to the Akkadian *zikaru*, "man" (Brünnow No. 5707), or possibly *rabû*, "great" (Brünnow No. 5704). Among various equivalents, the preference is to be given to *itlu*, "hero." The determinative for deity stamps the person so designated as deified, or as in part divine, and this is in accord with the express statement in the Assyrian version of the Gilgamesh Epic which describes the hero as

"Two-thirds god and one-third human."44

Gish is, therefore, the hero-god *par excellence*; and this shows that we are not dealing with a genuine proper name, but rather with a descriptive attribute. Proper names are not formed in this way, either in Sumerian or Akkadian. Now what relation does this form Gish bear to

as the name of the hero is invariably written in the Assyrian version, the form which was at first read ^{d}Iz-tu-bar or ^{d}Gish-du-bar by scholars, until Pinches found in a neo-Babylonian syllabary45 the equation of it with Gi-il-ga-mesh? Pinches' discovery pointed conclusively to the popular pronunciation of the hero's name as Gilgamesh; and since Aelian (*De natura Animalium* XII, 2) mentions a Babylonian personage Gilgamos (though what he tells us of Gilgamos does not appear in our Epic, but seems to apply to Etana, another figure of Babylonian mythology), there seemed to be no further reason to question that the problem had been solved. Besides, in a later Syriac list of Babylonian kings found in the Scholia of Theodor bar Koni, the name גלמגום with a variant גמיגמוס occurs,46 and it is evident that we have here again the Gi-il-ga-mesh, discovered by Pinches. The existence of an old Babylonian hero Gilgamesh who was likewise a king is thus established, as well as his identification with

It is evident that we cannot read this name as Iz-tu-bar or Gish-du-bar, but that we must read the first sign as Gish and the third as Mash, while for the second we must assume a reading Gìn or Gi. This would give us Gish-gì(n)-mash which is clearly again (like En-ki-dú) not an etymological writing but a *phonetic* one, intended to convey an *approach* to the popular pronunciation. Gi-il-ga-mesh might well be merely a variant for Gish-ga-mesh, or *vice versa*, and this would come close to Gish-gi-mash. Now, when we have a name the pronunciation of which is not definite but approximate, and which is written in various ways, the probabilities are that the name is foreign. A foreign name might naturally be spelled in various ways. The Epic in the Assyrian version clearly depicts ^{d}Gish-gì(n)-mash as a conqueror of Erech, who forces the people into subjection, and whose autocratic rule leads the people of Erech to implore the goddess Aruru to create a rival to him who may withstand him. In response to this appeal ^{d}Enkidu is formed out of dust by Aruru and eventually brought to Erech.47 Gish-gì(n)-mash or Gilgamesh is therefore in all probability a foreigner; and the simplest solution suggested by the existence of the two forms (1) Gish in the old Babylonian version and (2) Gish-gì(n)-mash in the Assyrian version, is to regard the former as an abbreviation, which seemed appropriate, because the short name conveyed the idea of the "hero" *par excellence*. If Gish-gì(n)-mash is a foreign name, one would think in the first instance of Sumerian; but here we encounter a difficulty in the circumstance that outside of the Epic this conqueror and ruler of Erech appears in quite a different form, namely, as ^{d}Gish-bil-ga-mesh, with ^{d}Gish-gibil(or bil)-ga-mesh and ^{d}Gish-bil-ge-mesh as variants.48 In the remarkable list of partly mythological and partly historical dynasties, published by Poebel,49 the fifth member of the first dynasty of Erech appears as ^{d}Gish-bil-ga-mesh; and similarly in an inscription of the days of Sin-gamil, ^{d}Gish-bil-ga-mesh is mentioned as the builder of the wall of Erech.50 Moreover, in the several fragments of the Sumerian version of the Epic we have invariably the form ^{d}Gish-bil-ga-mesh. It is evident, therefore, that this is the genuine form of the name in Sumerian and presumably, therefore, the oldest form. By way of further confirmation we have in the syllabary above referred to, CT, XVIII, 30, 6–8, three designations of our hero, viz:

1. ^{d}Gish-gibil(or bíl)-ga-mesh

2. *muḳ-tab-lu* ("warrior")

3. *a-lik pa-na* ("leader")

All three designations are set down as the equivalent of the Sumerian Esigga imin i.e., "the seven-fold hero."

Of the same general character is the equation in another syllabary:51

Esigga-tuk and its equivalent Gish-tuk = "the one who is a hero."

Furthermore, the name occurs frequently in "Temple" documents of the Ur dynasty in the form ^{d}Gish-bil-ga-mesh52 with ^{d}Gish-bil-gi(n)-mesh as a variant.53 In a list of deities (*CT* XXV, 28, K 7659) we likewise encounter ^{d}Gish-gibil(or bíl)-ga-mesh, and lastly in a syllabary we have the equation54

^{d}Gish-gi-mas-[si?] = ^{d}Gish-bil-[ga-mesh].

The variant Gish-gibil for Gish-bil may be disposed of readily, in view of the frequent confusion or interchange of the two signs Bil (Brünnow No. 4566) and Gibil or Bíl (Brünnow No. 4642) which has also the value Gi (Brünnow 4641), so that we might also read Gish-gi-ga-mesh. Both signs convey the idea of "fire," "renew," etc.; both revert to the picture of flames of fire, in the one case with a bowl (or some such obiect) above it, in the other the flames issuing apparently from a torch.55 The meaning of the name is not affected whether we read ^{d}Gish-bil-ga-mesh or ^{d}Gish-gibil(or bíl)-ga-mesh, for the middle element in the latter case being identical with the fire-god, written ^{d}Bil-gi and to be pronounced in the inverted form as Gibil with *-ga* (or *ge*) as the phonetic complement; it is equivalent, therefore, to the writing bil-ga in the former case. Now Gish-gibil or Gish-bíl conveys the idea of *abu*, "father" (Brünnow No. 5713), just as Bil (Brünnow No. 4579) has this meaning, while Pa-gibil-(ga) or Pa-bíl-ga is *abu abi*, "grandfather."56 This meaning may be derived from Gibil, as also from Bíl = *išatu*, "fire," then *eššu*, "new," then *abu*, "father," as the renewer or creator. Gish with Bíl or Gibil would, therefore, be "the father-man" or "the father-hero," i.e., again the hero *par excellence*, the original hero, just as in Hebrew and Arabic *ab* is used in this way.57 The syllable *ga* being a phonetic complement, the element *mesh* is to be taken by itself and to be explained, as Poebel suggested, as "hero" (*itlu*. Brünnow No. 5967).

We would thus obtain an entirely artificial combination, "man (or hero), father, hero," which would simply convey in an emphatic manner the idea of the *Ur-held*, the original hero, the father of heroes as it were—practically the same idea, therefore, as the one conveyed by Gish alone, as the hero *par excellence*. Our investigation thus leads us to a substantial identity between Gish and the longer form Gish-bil(or bíl)-ga-mesh, and the former might, therefore, well be used as an abbreviation of the latter. Both the shorter and the longer forms are *descriptive epithets* based on naive folk etymology, rather than personal names, just as in the designation of our hero as *muktablu*, the "fighter," or as *âlik pâna*, "the leader," or as *Esigga imin*, "the seven-fold hero," or *Esigga tuk*, "the one who is a hero," are descriptive epithets, and as Atra-ḫasis, "the very wise one," is such an epithet for the hero of the deluge story. The case is different with Gi-il-ga-mesh, or Gish-gì(n)-mash, which represent the popular and actual pronunciation of the name, or at least the *approach* to such pronunciation. Such forms, stripped as they are of all artificiality, impress one as genuine names. The conclusion to which we are thus led is that Gish-bil(or bíl)-ga-mesh is a play upon the genuine name, to convey to those to whom the real name, as that of a foreigner, would suggest no meaning an interpretation *fitting in with his character*. In other words, Gish-bil-ga-mesh is a "Sumerianized" form of the name, introduced into the Sumerian version of the tale which became a folk-possession in the Euphrates Valley. Such plays upon names to suggest the character of an individual or some incident are familiar to us from the narratives in Genesis.58 They do not constitute genuine etymologies and are rarely of use in leading to a correct etymology. Reuben, e.g., certainly does not mean "Yahweh has seen my affliction," which the mother is supposed to have exclaimed at the birth (Genesis 29, 32), with a play upon *ben* and *be'onyi*, any more than Judah means "I praise Yahweh" (v. 35), though it does contain the divine name (*Yehô*) as an element. The play on the name may be close or remote, as long as it fulfills its function of *suggesting* an etymology that is complimentary or appropriate.

In this way, an artificial division and at the same time a distortion of a foreign name like Gilgamesh into several elements, Gish-bil-ga-mesh, is no more violent than, for example, the explanation of Issachar or rather Issaschar as "God has given my hire" (Genesis 30, 18) with a play upon the element *s^{e}char*, and as though the name were to be divided into *Yah* ("God") and *s^{e}char* ("hire"); or the popular name of Alexander among the Arabs as *Zu'l Karnaini*, "the possessor of the two horns." with a suggestion of his conquest of two hemispheres, or what not.59 The element Gil in Gilgamesh would be regarded as a contraction of Gish-bil or gi-bil, in order to furnish the meaning "father-hero," or Gil might be looked upon as a variant for Gish, which would give us the "phonetic" form in the Assyrian version ^{d}Gish-gi-mash,60 as well as such a variant writing ^{d}Gish-gi-mas-(si). Now a name like Gilgamesh, upon which we may definitely settle as coming closest to the genuine form, certainly impresses one as foreign, i.e., it is neither Sumerian nor Akkadian; and we have already suggested that the circumstance that the hero of the Epic is portrayed as a conqueror of Erech, and a rather ruthless one at that, points to a tradition of an invasion of the Euphrates Valley as the background for the episode in the first tablet of the series. Now it is significant that many of the names in the "mythical" dynasties, as they appear in Poebel's list,61 are likewise foreign, such as Mes-ki-in-ga-še-ir, son of the god Shamash (and the founder of the "mythical" dynasty of Erech of which ^{d}Gish-bil-ga-mesh is the fifth member),62 and En-me-ir-kár his son. In a still earlier "mythical" dynasty, we encounter names like Ga-lu-mu-um, Zu-ga-gi-ib, Ar-pi, E-ta-na,63 which are distinctly foreign, while such names as En-me(n)-nun-na and Bar-sal-nun-na strike one again as "Sumerianized" names rather than as genuine Sumerian formations.64

Some of these names, as Galumum, Arpi and Etana, are so Amoritic in appearance, that one may hazard the conjecture of their western origin. May Gilgamesh likewise belong to the Amurru65 region, or does he represent a foreigner from the East in contrast to Enkidu, whose name, we have seen, may have been Baal-Ṭôb in the West, with which region he is according to the Epic so familiar? It must be confessed that the second element *ga-mesh* would fit in well with a Semitic origin for the name, for the element impresses one as the participial form of a Semitic stem g-m-š, just as in the second element of Meskin-gašer we have such a form. Gil might then be the name of a West-Semitic deity.

Such conjectures, however, can for the present not be substantiated, and we must content ourselves with the conclusion that Gilgamesh as the real name of the hero, or at least the form which comes closest to the real name, points to a foreign origin for the hero, and that such forms as ^{d}Gish-bil-ga-mesh and ^{d}Gish-bíl-gi-mesh and other variants are "Sumerianized" forms for which an artificial etymology was brought forward to convey the idea of the "original hero" or the hero *par excellence.* By means of this "play" on the name, which reverts to the compilers of the Sumerian version of the Epic, Gilgamesh was converted into a Sumerian figure, just as the name Enkidu may have been introduced as a Sumerian translation of his Amoritic name. ^{d}Gish at all events is an abbreviated form of the "Sumerianized" name, introduced by the compilers of the earliest Akkadian version, which was produced naturally under the influence of the Sumerian version. Later, as the Epic continued to grow, a phonetic writing was introduced, ^{d}Gish-gi-mash, which is in a measure a compromise between the genuine name and the "Sumerianized" form, but at the same time an *approach* to the real pronunciation.

Next to the new light thrown upon the names and original character of the two main figures of the Epic, one of the chief points of interest in the Pennsylvania fragment is the proof that it furnishes for a striking resemblance of the two heroes, Gish and Enkidu, to one another. In interpreting the dream of Gish, his mother. Ninsun, lays stress upon the fact that the dream portends the coming of someone who is like Gish, "born in the field and reared in the mountain" (lines 18–19). Both, therefore, are shown by this description to have come to Babylonia from a mountainous region, i.e., they are foreigners; and in the case of Enkidu we have seen that the mountain in all probability refers to a region in the West, while the same may also be the case with Gish. The resemblance of the two heroes to one another extends to their personal appearance. When Enkidu appears on the streets of Erech, the people are struck by this resemblance. They remark that he is "like Gish," though "shorter in stature" (lines 179–180). Enkidu is described as a rival or counterpart.66

This relationship between the two is suggested also by the Assyrian version. In the creation of Enkidu by Aruru, the people urge the goddess to create the "counterpart" (*zikru*) of Gilgamesh, someone who will be like him (*ma-ši-il*) (Tablet I, 2, 31). Enkidu not only comes from the mountain,67 but the mountain is specifically designated as his birth-place (I, 4, 2), precisely as in the Pennsylvania tablet, while in another passage he is also described, as in our tablet, as "born in the field."68 Still more significant is the designation of Gilgamesh as the *talimu*, "younger brother," of Enkidu.69 In accord with this, we find Gilgamesh in his lament over Enkidu describing him as a "younger brother" (*ku-ta-ni*);70 and again in the last tablet of the Epic, Gilgamesh is referred to as the "brother" of Enkidu.71 This close relationship reverts to the Sumerian version, for the Constantinople fragment (Langdon, above, p. 13) begins with the designation of Gish-bil-ga-mesh as "his brother." By "his" no doubt Enkidu is meant. Likewise in the Sumerian text published by Zimmern (above, p. 13) Gilgamesh appears as the brother of Enkidu (rev. 1, 17).

Turning to the numerous representations of Gilgamesh and Enkidu on Seal Cylinders,72 we find this resemblance of the two heroes to each other strikingly confirmed. Both are represented as bearded, with the strands arranged in the same fashion. The face in both cases is broad, with curls protruding at the side of the head, though at times these curls are lacking in the case of Enkidu. What is particularly striking is to find Gilgamesh generally *a little taller* than Enkidu, thus bearing out the statement in the Pennsylvania tablet that Enkidu is "shorter in stature." There are, to be sure, also some distinguishing marks between the two. Thus Enkidu is generally represented with animal hoofs, but not always.73 Enkidu is commonly portrayed with the horns of a bison, but again this sign is wanting in quite a number of instances.74 The hoofs and the horns mark the period when Enkidu lived with animals and much like an animal. Most remarkable, however, of all are cylinders on which we find the two heroes almost exactly alike as, for example, Ward No. 199 where two figures, the one a duplicate of the other (except that one is just a shade taller), are in conflict with each other. Dr. Ward was puzzled by this representation and sets it down as a "fantastic" scene in which "each Gilgamesh is stabbing the other." In the light of the Pennsylvania tablet, this scene is clearly the conflict between the two heroes described in column 6, preliminary to their forming a friendship. Even in the realm of myth the human experience holds good that there is nothing like a good fight as a basis for a subsequent alliance. The fragment describes this conflict as a furious one in which Gilgamesh is worsted, and his wounded pride assuaged by the generous victor, who comforts his vanquished enemy by the assurance that he was destined for something higher than to be a mere

"Hercules." He was singled out for the exercise of royal authority. True to the description of the two heroes in the Pennsylvania tablet as alike, one the counterpart of the other, the seal cylinder portrays them almost exactly alike, as alike as two brothers could possibly be; with just enough distinction to make it clear on close inspection that two figures are intended and not one repeated for the sake of symmetry. There are slight variations in the manner in which the hair is worn, and slightly varying expressions of the face, just enough to make it evident that the one is intended for Gilgamesh and the other for Enkidu. When, therefore, in another specimen, No. 173, we find a Gilgamesh holding his counterpart by the legs, it is merely another aspect of the fight between the two heroes, one of whom is intended to represent Enkidu, and not, as Dr. Ward supposed, a grotesque repetition of Gilgamesh.75

The description of Enkidu in the Pennsylvania tablet as a parallel figure to Gilgamesh leads us to a consideration of the relationship of the two figures to one another. Many years ago it was pointed out that the Gilgamesh Epic was a composite tale in which various stories of an independent origin had been combined and brought into more or less artificial connection with the *heros eponymos* of southern Babylonia.76 We may now go a step further and point out that not only is Enkidu originally an entirely independent figure, having no connection with Gish or Gilgamesh, but that the latter is really depicted in the Epic as the counterpart of Enkidu, a reflection who has been given the traits of extraordinary physical power that belong to Enkidu. This is shown in the first place by the fact that in the encounter it is Enkidu who triumphs over Gilgamesh. The entire analysis of the episode of the meeting between the two heroes as given by Gressmann77 must be revised. It is not Enkidu who is terrified and who is warned against the encounter. It is Gilgamesh who, during the night on his way from the house in which the goddess Ishḫara lies, encounters Enkidu on the highway. Enkidu "blocks the path"78 of Gilgamesh. He prevents Gilgamesh from re-entering the house,79 and the two attack each other "like oxen."80 They grapple with each other, and Enkidu forces Gilgamesh to the ground. Enkidu is, therefore, the real hero whose traits of physical prowess are afterwards transferred to Gilgamesh.

Similarly in the next episode, the struggle against Ḫuwawa, the Yale tablet makes it clear that in the original form of the tale Enkidu is the real hero. All warn Gish against the undertaking—the elders of Erech,

Enkidu, and also the workmen. "Why dost thou desire to do this?"81 they say to him. "Thou art young, and thy heart carries thee away. Thou knowest not what thou proposest to do."82 This part of the incident is now better known to us through the latest fragment of the Assyrian version discovered and published by King.83 The elders say to Gilgamesh:

"Do not trust, O Gilgamesh, in thy strength!

Be warned(?) against trusting to thy attack!

The one who goes before will save his companion,84

He who has foresight will save his friend.85

Let Enkidu go before thee.

He knows the roads to the cedar forest;

He is skilled in battle and has seen fight."

Gilgamesh is sufficiently impressed by this warning to invite Enkidu to accompany him on a visit to his mother, Ninsun, for the purpose of receiving her counsel.86

It is only after Enkidu, who himself hesitates and tries to dissuade Gish, decides to accompany the latter that the elders of Erech are reconciled and encourage Gish for the fray. The two in concert proceed against Ḫuwawa. Gilgamesh alone cannot carry out the plan. Now when a tale thus associates two figures in one deed, one of the two has been added to the original tale. In the present case there can be little doubt that Enkidu, without whom Gish cannot proceed, who is specifically described as "acquainted with the way … to the entrance of the forest"87 in which Ḫuwawa dwells is the *original* vanquisher. Naturally, the Epic aims to conceal this fact as much as possible *ad majorem gloriam* of Gilgamesh. It tries to put the one who became the favorite hero into the foreground. Therefore, in both the Babylonian and the Assyrian version Enkidu is represented as hesitating, and Gilgamesh as determined to go ahead. Gilgamesh, in fact, accuses Enkidu of cowardice and boldly declares that he will proceed even though failure stare him in the face.88 Traces of the older view, however, in which Gilgamesh is the one for whom one fears the outcome, crop out; as, for example, in the complaint of Gilgamesh's mother to Shamash that the latter has stirred the heart of her son to take the distant way to Ḫu(m)baba,

"To a fight unknown to him, he advances,

An expedition unknown to him he undertakes."89

Ninsun evidently fears the consequences when her son informs her of his intention and asks her counsel. The answer of Shamash is not preserved, but no doubt it was of a reassuring character, as was the answer of the Sun-god to Gish's appeal and prayer as set forth in the Yale tablet.90

Again, as a further indication that Enkidu is the real conqueror of Ḫuwawa, we find the coming contest revealed to Enkidu no less than three times in dreams, which Gilgamesh interprets.91 Since the person who dreams is always the one to whom the dream applies, we may see in these dreams a further trace of the primary rôle originally assigned to Enkidu.

Another exploit which, according to the Assyrian version, the two heroes perform in concert is the killing of a bull, sent by Anu at the instance of Ishtar to avenge an insult offered to the goddess by Gilgamesh, who rejects her offer of marriage. In the fragmentary description of the contest with the bull, we find Enkidu "seizing" the monster by "its tail."92

That Enkidu originally played the part of the slayer is also shown by the statement that it is he who insults Ishtar by throwing a piece of the carcass into the goddess' face,93 adding also an insulting speech; and this despite the fact that Ishtar in her rage accuses Gilgamesh of killing the bull.94 It is thus evident that the Epic alters the original character of the episodes in order to find a place for Gilgamesh, with the further desire to assign to the latter the *chief* rôle. Be it noted also that Enkidu, not Gilgamesh, is punished for the insult to Ishtar. Enkidu must therefore in the original form of the episode have been the guilty party, who is stricken with mortal disease as a punishment to which after twelve days he succumbs.95 In view of this, we may supply the name of Enkidu in the little song introduced at the close of the encounter with the bull, and not Gilgamesh as has hitherto been done.

"Who is distinguished among the heroes?

Who is glorious among men?

[Enkidu] is distinguished among heroes,

[Enkidu] is glorious among men."96

Finally, the killing of lions is directly ascribed to Enkidu in the Pennsylvania tablet:

"Lions he attacked

* * * * *

Lions he overcame"97

whereas Gilgamesh appears to be afraid of lions. On his long search for Utnapishtim he says:

"On reaching the entrance of the mountain at night

I saw lions and was afraid."98

He prays to Sin and Ishtar to protect and save him. When, therefore, in another passage some one celebrates Gilgamesh as the one who overcame the "guardian," who dispatched Ḫu(m)baba in the cedar forest, who killed lions and overthrew the bull,99 we have the completion of the process which transferred to Gilgamesh exploits and powers which originally belonged to Enkidu, though ordinarily the process stops short at making Gilgamesh a *sharer* in the exploits; with the natural tendency, to be sure, to enlarge the share of the favorite.

We can now understand why the two heroes are described in the Pennsylvania tablet as alike, as born in the same place, aye, as brothers. Gilgamesh in the Epic is merely a reflex of Enkidu. The latter is the real hero and presumably, therefore, the older figure.100 Gilgamesh resembles Enkidu, because he *is* originally Enkidu. The "resemblance" *motif* is merely the manner in which in the course of the partly popular, partly literary transfer, the recollection is preserved that Enkidu is the original, and Gilgamesh the copy.

The artificiality of the process which brings the two heroes together is apparent in the dreams of Gilgamesh which are interpreted by his mother as portending the coming of Enkidu. Not the conflict is foreseen, but the subsequent close association, naïvely described as due to the personal charm which Enkidu exercises, which will lead Gilgamesh to fall in love with the one whom he is to meet. The two will become one, like man and wife.

On the basis of our investigations, we are now in a position to reconstruct in part the cycle of episodes that once formed part of an Enkidu Epic. The fight between Enkidu and Gilgamesh, in which the former is the victor, is typical of the kind of tales told of Enkidu. He is the real prototype of the Greek Hercules. He slays lions, he overcomes a powerful opponent dwelling in the forests of Lebanon, he kills the bull, and he finally succumbs to disease sent as a punishment by an angry goddess. The death of Enkidu naturally formed the close of the Enkidu Epic, which in its original form may, of course, have included other exploits besides those taken over into the Gilgamesh Epic.

There is another aspect of the figure of Enkidu which is brought forward in the Pennsylvania tablet more clearly than had hitherto been the case. Many years ago attention was called to certain striking resemblances between Enkidu and the figure of the first man as described in the early chapters of Genesis.101 At that time we had merely the Assyrian version of the Gilgamesh Epic at our disposal, and the main point of contact was the description of Enkidu living with the animals, drinking and feeding like an animal, until a woman is brought to him with whom he engages in sexual intercourse. This suggested that Enkidu was a picture of primeval man, while the woman reminded one of Eve, who when she is brought to Adam becomes his helpmate and inseparable companion. The Biblical tale stands, of course, on a much higher level, and is introduced, as are other traditions and tales of primitive times, in the style of a parable to convey certain religious teachings. For all that, suggestions of earlier conceptions crop out in the picture of Adam surrounded by animals to which he assigns names. Such a phrase as "there was no helpmate corresponding to him" becomes intelligible on the supposition of an existing tradition or belief, that man once lived and, indeed, cohabited with animals. The tales in the early chapters of Genesis must rest on very early popular traditions, which have been cleared of mythological and other objectionable features in order to adapt them to the purpose of the Hebrew compilers, to serve as a medium for illustrating certain religious teachings regarding man's place in nature and his higher destiny. From the resemblance between Enkidu and Adam it does not, of course, follow that the latter is modelled upon the former, but only that both rest on similar traditions of the condition under which men lived in primeval days prior to the beginnings of human culture.

We may now pass beyond these general indications and recognize in the story of Enkidu as revealed by the Pennsylvania tablet an attempt to trace the evolution of primitive man from low beginnings to the regular and orderly family life associated with advanced culture. The new tablet furnishes a further illustration for the surprisingly early tendency among the Babylonian *literati* to connect with popular tales teachings of a religious or ethical character. Just as the episode between Gilgamesh and the maiden Sabitum is made the occasion for introducing reflections on the inevitable fate of man to encounter death, so the meeting of Enkidu with the woman becomes the medium of impressing the lesson of human progress through the substitution of bread and wine for milk and water, through the institution of the family, and through work and the laying up of resources. This is the significance of the address to Enkidu in column 4 of the Pennsylvania tablet, even though certain expressions in it are somewhat obscure. The connection of the entire episode of Enkidu and the woman with Gilgamesh is very artificial; and it becomes much more intelligible if we disassociate it from its present entanglement in the Epic. In Gilgamesh's dream, portending the meeting with Enkidu, nothing is said of the woman who is the companion of the latter. The passage in which Enkidu is created by Aruru to oppose Gilgamesh102 betrays evidence of having been worked over in order to bring Enkidu into association with the longing of the people of Erech to get rid of a tyrannical character. The people in their distress appeal to Aruru to create a rival to Gilgamesh. In response,

"Aruru upon hearing this created a man of Anu in her heart."

Now this "man of Anu" cannot possibly be Enkidu, for the sufficient reason that a few lines further on Enkidu is described as an offspring of Ninib. Moreover, the being created is not a "counterpart" of Gilgamesh, but an animal-man, as the description that follows shows. We must separate lines 30–33 in which the creation of the "Anu man" is described from lines 34–41 in which the creation of Enkidu is narrated. Indeed, these lines strike one as the proper *beginning* of the original Enkidu story, which would naturally start out with his birth and end with his death. The description is clearly an account of the creation of the first man, in which capacity Enkidu is brought forward.

"Aruru washed her hands, broke off clay,

threw it on the field103

… created Enkidu, the hero, a lofty

offspring of the host of Ninib."104

The description of Enkidu follows, with his body covered with hair like an animal, and eating and drinking with the animals. There follows an episode105 which has no connection whatsoever with the Gilgamesh Epic, but which is clearly intended to illustrate how Enkidu came to abandon the life with the animals. A hunter sees Enkidu and is amazed at the strange sight—an animal and yet a man. Enkidu, as though resenting his condition, becomes enraged at the sight of the hunter, and the latter goes to his father and tells him of the strange creature whom he is unable to catch. In reply, the father advises his son to take a woman with him when next he goes out on his pursuit, and to have the woman remove her dress in the presence of Enkidu, who will then approach her, and after intercourse with her will abandon the animals among whom he lives. By this device he will catch the strange creature. Lines 14–18 of column 3 in the first tablet in which the father of the hunter refers to Gilgamesh must be regarded as a later insertion, a part of the reconstruction of the tale to connect the episode with Gilgamesh. The advice of the father to his son, the hunter, begins, line 19,

"Go my hunter, take with thee a woman."

In the reconstructed tale, the father tells his son to go to Gilgamesh to relate to him the strange appearance of the animal-man; but there is clearly no purpose in this, as is shown by the fact that when the hunter does so, Gilgamesh makes *precisely the same speech* as does the father of the hunter. Lines 40–44 of column 3, in which Gilgamesh is represented as speaking to the hunter form a complete *doublet* to lines 19–24, beginning

"Go, my hunter, take with thee a woman, etc."

and similarly the description of Enkidu appears twice, lines 2–12 in an address of the hunter to his father, and lines 29–39 in the address of the hunter to Gilgamesh.

The artificiality of the process of introducing Gilgamesh into the episode is revealed by this awkward and entirely meaningless repetition. We may therefore reconstruct the first two scenes in the Enkidu Epic as follows:106

Tablet I, col. 2, 34–35: Creation of Enkidu by Aruru.

36–41: Description of Enkidu's hairy body and of his life with the animals.

42–50: The hunter sees Enkidu, who shows his anger, as also his woe, at his condition.

3, 1–12: The hunter tells his father of the strange being who pulls up the traps which the hunter digs, and who tears the nets so that the hunter is unable to catch him or the animals.

19–24: The father of the hunter advises his son on his next expedition to take a woman with him in order to lure the strange being from his life with the animals.

Line 25, beginning "On the advice of his father," must have set forth, in the original form of the episode, how the hunter procured the woman and took her with him to meet Enkidu.

Column 4 gives in detail the meeting between the two, and naïvely describes how the woman exposes her charms to Enkidu, who is captivated by her and stays with her six days and seven nights. The animals see the change in Enkidu and run away from him. He has been transformed through the woman. So far the episode. In the Assyrian version there follows an address of the woman to Enkidu beginning (col. 4, 34):

"Beautiful art thou, Enkidu, like a god art thou."

We find her urging him to go with her to Erech, there to meet Gilgamesh and to enjoy the pleasures of city life with plenty of beautiful maidens. Gilgamesh, she adds, will expect Enkidu, for the coming of the latter to Erech has been foretold in a dream. It is evident that here we have again the later transformation of the Enkidu Epic in order to bring the two heroes together. Will it be considered too bold if we assume that in the original form the address of the woman and the construction of the episode were such as we find preserved in part in columns 2 to 4 of the Pennsylvania tablet, which forms part of the new material that can now be added to the Epic? The address of the woman begins in line 51 of the Pennsylvania tablet:

"I gaze upon thee, Enkidu, like a god art thou."

This corresponds to the line in the Assyrian version (I, 4, 34) as given above, just as lines 52–53:

"Why with the cattle

Dost thou roam across the field?"

correspond to I, 4, 35, of the Assyrian version. There follows in both the old Babylonian and the Assyrian version the appeal of the woman to Enkidu, to allow her to lead him to Erech where Gilgamesh dwells (Pennsylvania tablet lines 54–61 = Assyrian version I, 4, 36–39); but in the Pennsylvania tablet we now have a *second* speech (lines 62–63) beginning like the first one with *al-ka*, "come:"

"Come, arise from the accursed ground."

Enkidu consents, and now the woman takes off her garments and clothes the naked Enkidu, while putting another garment on herself. She takes hold of his hand and leads him to the sheepfolds (not to Erech!!), where bread and wine are placed before him. Accustomed hitherto to sucking milk with cattle, Enkidu does not know what to do with the strange food until encouraged and instructed by the woman. The entire third column is taken up with this introduction of Enkidu to civilized life in a pastoral community, and the scene ends with Enkidu becoming a guardian of flocks. Now all this has nothing to do with Gilgamesh, and clearly sets forth an entirely different idea from the one embodied in the meeting of the two heroes. In the original Enkidu tale, the animal-man is looked upon as the type of a primitive savage, and the point of the tale is to illustrate in the naïve manner characteristic of folklore the evolution to the higher form of pastoral life. This aspect of the incident is, therefore, to be separated from the other phase which has as its chief *motif* the bringing of the two heroes together.

We now obtain, thanks to the new section revealed by the Pennsylvania tablet, a further analogy107 with the story of Adam and Eve, but with this striking difference, that whereas in the Babylonian tale the woman is the medium leading man to the higher life, in the Biblical story the woman is the tempter who brings misfortune to man. This contrast is, however, not inherent in the Biblical story, but due to the point of view of the Biblical writer, who is somewhat pessimistically inclined and looks upon primitive life, when man went naked and lived in a garden, eating of fruits that grew of themselves, as the blessed life in contrast to advanced culture which leads to agriculture and necessitates hard work as the means of securing one's substance. Hence the woman through whom Adam eats of the tree of knowledge and becomes conscious of being naked is looked upon as an evil tempter, entailing the loss of the primeval life of bliss in a gorgeous Paradise. The Babylonian point of view is optimistic. The change to civilized life—involving the wearing of clothes and the eating of food that is cultivated (bread and wine) is looked upon as an advance. Hence the woman is viewed as the medium of raising man to a higher level. The feature common to the Biblical and Babylonian tales is the attachment of a lesson to early folk-tales. The story of Adam and Eve,108 as the story of Enkidu and the woman, is told *with a purpose.* Starting with early traditions of men's primitive life on earth, that may have arisen independently, Hebrew and Babylonian writers diverged, each group going its own way, each reflecting the particular point of view from which the evolution of human society was viewed.

Leaving the analogy between the Biblical and Babylonian tales aside, the main point of value for us in the Babylonian story of Enkidu and the woman is the proof furnished by the analysis, made possible through the Pennsylvania tablet, that the tale can be separated from its subsequent connection with Gilgamesh. We can continue this process of separation in the fourth column, where the woman instructs Enkidu in the further duty of living his life with the woman decreed for him, to raise a family, to engage in work, to build cities and to gather resources. All this is looked upon in the same optimistic spirit as marking progress, whereas the Biblical writer, consistent with his point of view, looks upon work as a curse, and makes Cain, the murderer, also the founder of cities. The step to the higher forms of life is not an advance according to the J document. It is interesting to note that even the phrase the "cursed ground" occurs in both the Babylonian and Biblical tales; but whereas in the latter (Gen. 3, 17) it is because of the hard work entailed in raising the products of the earth that the ground is cursed, in the former (lines 62–63) it is the place in which Enkidu lives *before* he advances to the dignity of human life that is "cursed," and which he is asked to leave. Adam is expelled from Paradise as a punishment, whereas Enkidu is implored to leave it as a necessary step towards *progress* to a higher form of existence. The contrast between the Babylonian and the Biblical writer extends to the view taken of viniculture. The Biblical writer (again the J document) looks upon Noah's drunkenness as a disgrace. Noah loses his sense of shame and uncovers himself (Genesis 9, 21), whereas in the Babylonian description Enkidu's jolly spirit after he has drunk seven jars of wine meets with approval. The Biblical point of view is that he who drinks wine becomes drunk;[109] the Babylonian says, if you drink wine you become happy.[110]

If the thesis here set forth of the original character and import of the episode of Enkidu with the woman is correct, we may again regard lines 149–153 of the Pennsylvania tablet, in which Gilgamesh is introduced, as a later addition to bring the two heroes into association. The episode in its original form ended with the introduction of Enkidu first to pastoral life, and then to the still higher city life with regulated forms of social existence.

Now, to be sure, this Enkidu has little in common with the Enkidu who is described as a powerful warrior, a Hercules, who kills lions, overcomes the giant Ḫuwawa, and dispatches a great bull, but it is the nature of folklore everywhere to attach to traditions about a favorite hero all kinds of tales with which originally he had nothing to do. Enkidu, as such a favorite, is viewed also as the type of primitive man,[111] and so there arose gradually an Epic which began with his birth, pictured him as half-animal half-man, told how he emerged from this state, how he became civilized, was clothed, learned to eat food and drink wine, how he shaved off the hair with which his body was covered,[112] anointed himself—in short,

"He became manlike."[113]

Thereupon he is taught his duties as a husband, is introduced to the work of building, and to laying aside supplies, and the like. The fully-developed and full-fledged hero then engages in various exploits, of which *some* are now embodied in the Gilgamesh Epic. Who this Enkidu was, we are not in a position to determine, but the suggestion has been thrown out above that he is a personage foreign to Babylonia, that his home appears to be in the undefined Amurru district, and that he conquers that district. The original tale of Enkidu, if this view be correct, must therefore have been carried to the Euphrates Valley, at a very remote period, with one of the migratory waves that brought a western people as invaders into Babylonia. Here the tale was combined with stories current of another hero, Gilgamesh—perhaps also of Western origin—whose conquest of Erech likewise represents an invasion of Babylonia. The center of the Gilgamesh tale was Erech, and in the process of combining the stories of Enkidu and Gilgamesh, Enkidu is brought to Erech and the two perform exploits in common. In such a combination, the aim would be to utilize all the incidents of *both* tales. The woman who accompanies Enkidu, therefore, becomes the medium of bringing the two heroes together. The story of the evolution of primitive man to civilized life is transformed into the tale of Enkidu's removal to Erech, and elaborated with all kinds of details, among which we have, as perhaps embodying a genuine historical tradition, the encounter of the two heroes.

Before passing on, we have merely to note the very large part taken in both the old Babylonian and the Assyrian version by the struggle against Ḫuwawa. The entire Yale tablet—forming, as we have seen, the third of the series—is taken up with the preparation for the struggle, and with the repeated warnings given to Gilgamesh against the dangerous undertaking. The fourth tablet must have recounted the struggle itself, and it is not improbable that this episode extended into the fifth tablet, since in the Assyrian version this is the case. The elaboration of the story is in itself an argument in favor of assuming some historical background for it—the recollection of the conquest of Amurru by some powerful warrior; and we have seen that this conquest must be ascribed to Enkidu and not to Gilgamesh.

If, now, Enkidu is not only the older figure but the one who is the real hero of the most notable episode in the Gilgamesh Epic; if, furthermore, Enkidu is the Hercules who kills lions and dispatches the bull sent by an enraged goddess, what becomes of Gilgamesh? What is left for him?

In the first place, he is definitely the conqueror of Erech. He builds the wall of Erech,114 and we may assume that the designation of the city as *Uruk supûri*, "the walled Erech,"115 rests upon this tradition. He is also associated with the great temple Eanna, "the heavenly house," in Erech. To Gilgamesh belongs also the unenviable tradition of having exercised his rule in Erech so harshly that the people are impelled to implore Aruru to create a rival who may rid the district of the cruel tyrant, who is described as snatching sons and daughters from their families, and in other ways terrifying the population—an early example of "Schrecklichkeit." Tablets II to V inclusive of the Assyrian version being taken up with the Ḫuwawa episode, modified with a view of bringing the two heroes together, we come at once to the sixth tablet, which tells the story of how the goddess Ishtar wooed Gilgamesh, and of the latter's rejection of her advances. This tale is distinctly a nature myth. The attempt of Gressmann116 to find some historical background to the episode is a failure. The goddess Ishtar symbolizes the earth which woos the sun in the spring, but whose love is fatal, for after a few months the sun's power begins to wane. Gilgamesh, who in incantation hymns is invoked in terms which show that he was conceived as a sun-god,117 recalls to the goddess how she changed her lovers into animals, like Circe of Greek mythology, and brought them to grief. Enraged at Gilgamesh's insult to her vanity, she flies to her father Anu and cries for revenge. At this point the episode of the creation of the bull is introduced, but if the analysis above given is correct it is Enkidu who is the hero in dispatching the bull, and we must assume that the sickness with which Gilgamesh is smitten is the punishment sent by Anu to avenge the insult to his daughter. This sickness symbolizes the waning strength of the sun after midsummer is past. The sun recedes from the earth, and this was pictured in the myth as the sun-god's rejection of Ishtar; Gilgamesh's fear of death marks the approach of the winter season, when the sun appears to have lost its vigor completely and is near to death. The entire episode is, therefore, a nature myth, symbolical of the passing of spring to midsummer and then to the bare season. The myth has been attached to Gilgamesh as a favorite figure, and then woven into a pattern with the episode of Enkidu and the bull. The bull episode can be detached from the nature myth without any loss to the symbolism of the tale of Ishtar and Gilgamesh.

As already suggested, with Enkidu's death after this conquest of the bull the original Enkidu Epic came to an end. In order to connect Gilgamesh with Enkidu, the former is represented as sharing in the struggle against the bull. Enkidu is punished with death, while Gilgamesh is smitten with disease. Since both shared equally in the guilt, the punishment should have been the same for both. The differentiation may be taken as an indication that Gilgamesh's disease has nothing to do with the bull episode, but is merely part of the nature myth.

Gilgamesh now begins a series of wanderings in search of the restoration of his vigor, and this *motif* is evidently a continuation of the nature myth to symbolize the sun's wanderings during the dark winter in the hope of renewed vigor with the coming of the spring. Professor Haupt's view is that the disease from which Gilgamesh is supposed to be suffering is of a venereal character, affecting the organs of reproduction. This would confirm the position here taken that the myth symbolizes the loss of the sun's vigor. The sun's rays are no longer strong enough to fertilize the earth. In accord with this, Gilgamesh's search for healing leads him to the dark regions118 in which the scorpion-men dwell. The terrors of the region symbolize the gloom of the winter season. At last Gilgamesh reaches a region of light again, described as a landscape situated at the sea. The maiden in control of this region bolts the gate against Gilgamesh's approach, but the latter forces his entrance. It is the picture of the sun-god bursting through the darkness, to emerge as the youthful reinvigorated sun-god of the spring.

Now with the tendency to attach to popular tales and nature myths lessons illustrative of current beliefs and aspirations, Gilgamesh's search for renewal of life is viewed as man's longing for eternal life. The sun-god's waning power after midsummer is past suggests man's growing weakness after the meridian of life has been left behind. Winter is death, and man longs to escape it. Gilgamesh's wanderings are used as illustration of this longing, and accordingly the search for life becomes also the quest for immortality. Can the precious boon of eternal life be achieved? Popular fancy created the figure of a favorite of the gods who had escaped a destructive deluge in which all mankind had perished.119 Gilgamesh hears of this favorite and determines to seek him out and learn from him the secret of eternal life. The deluge story, again a pure nature myth, symbolical of the rainy season which destroys all life in nature, is thus attached to the Epic. Gilgamesh after many adventures finds himself in the presence of the survivor of the Deluge who, although human, enjoys immortal life among the gods. He asks the survivor how he came to escape the common fate of mankind, and in reply Utnapishtim tells the story of the catastrophe that brought about universal destruction. The moral of the tale is obvious. Only those singled out by the special favor of the gods can hope to be removed to the distant "source of the streams" and live forever. The rest of mankind must face death as the end of life.

That the story of the Deluge is told in the eleventh tablet of the series, corresponding to the eleventh month, known as the month of "rain curse"[120] and marking the height of the rainy season, may be intentional, just as it may not be accidental that Gilgamesh's rejection of Ishtar is recounted in the sixth tablet, corresponding to the sixth month,[121] which marks the end of the summer season. The two tales may have formed part of a cycle of myths, distributed among the months of the year. The Gilgamesh Epic, however, does not form such a cycle. Both myths have been artificially attached to the adventures of the hero. For the deluge story we now have the definite proof for its independent existence, through Dr. Poebel's publication of a Sumerian text which embodies the tale,[122] and without any reference to Gilgamesh. Similarly, Scheil and Hilprecht have published fragments of deluge stories written in Akkadian and likewise without any connection with the Gilgamesh Epic.[123]

In the Epic the story leads to another episode attached to Gilgamesh, namely, the search for a magic plant growing in deep water, which has the power of restoring old age to youth. Utnapishtim, the survivor of the deluge, is moved through pity for Gilgamesh, worn out by his long wanderings. At the request of his wife, Utnapishtim decides to tell Gilgamesh of this plant, and he succeeds in finding it. He plucks it and decides to take it back to Erech so that all may enjoy the benefit, but on his way stops to bathe in a cool cistern. A serpent comes along and snatches the plant from him, and he is forced to return to Erech with his purpose unachieved. Man cannot hope, when old age comes on, to escape death as the end of everything.

Lastly, the twelfth tablet of the Assyrian version of the Gilgamesh Epic is of a purely didactic character, bearing evidence of having been added as a further illustration of the current belief that there is no escape from the nether world to which all must go after life has come to an end. Proper burial and suitable care of the dead represent all that can be done in order to secure a fairly comfortable rest for those who have passed out of this world. Enkidu is once more introduced into this episode. His shade is invoked by Gilgamesh and rises up out of the lower world to give a discouraging reply to Gilgamesh's request,

"Tell me, my friend, tell me, my friend,

The law of the earth which thou hast

experienced, tell me,"

The mournful message comes back:

"I cannot tell thee, my friend, I cannot tell."

Death is a mystery and must always remain such. The historical Gilgamesh has clearly no connection with the figure introduced into this twelfth tablet. Indeed, as already suggested, the Gilgamesh Epic must have ended with the return to Erech, as related at the close of the eleventh tablet. The twelfth tablet was added by some school-men of Babylonia (or perhaps of Assyria), purely for the purpose of conveying a summary of the teachings in regard to the fate of the dead. Whether these six episodes covering the sixth to the twelfth tablets, (1) the nature myth, (2) the killing of the divine bull, (3) the punishment of Gilgamesh and the death of Enkidu, (4) Gilgamesh's wanderings, (5) the Deluge, (6) the search for immortality, were all included at the time that the old Babylonian version was compiled cannot, of course, be determined until we have that version in a more complete form. Since the two tablets thus far recovered show that as early as 2000 B.C. the Enkidu tale had already been amalgamated with the current stories about Gilgamesh, and the endeavor made to transfer the traits of the former to the latter, it is eminently likely that the story of Ishtar's unhappy love adventure with Gilgamesh was included, as well as Gilgamesh's punishment and the death of Enkidu. With the evidence furnished by Meissner's fragment of a version of the old Babylonian revision and by our two tablets, of the early disposition to make popular tales the medium of illustrating current beliefs and the teachings of the temple schools, it may furthermore be concluded that the death of Enkidu and the punishment of Gilgamesh were utilized for didactic purposes in the old Babylonian version. On the other hand, the proof for the existence of the deluge story in the Hammurabi period and some centuries later, *independent* of any connection with the Gilgamesh Epic, raises the question whether in the old Babylonian version, of which our two tablets form a part, the deluge tale was already woven into the pattern of the Epic. At all events, till proof to the contrary is forthcoming, we may assume that the twelfth tablet of the Assyrian version, though also reverting to a Babylonian original, dates as the *latest* addition to the Epic from a period subsequent to 2000 B.C.; and that the same is probably the case with the eleventh tablet.

To sum up, there are four main currents that flow together in the Gilgamesh Epic even in its old Babylonian form: (1) the adventures of a mighty warrior Enkidu, resting perhaps on a faint tradition of the conquest of Amurru by the hero; (2) the more definite recollection of the exploits of a foreign invader of Babylonia by the name of Gilgamesh, whose home appears likewise to have been in the West;124 (3) nature myths and didactic tales transferred to Enkidu and Gilgamesh as popular figures; and (4) the process of weaving the traditions, exploits, myths and didactic tales together, in the course of which process Gilgamesh becomes the main hero, and Enkidu his companion.

Furthermore, our investigation has shown that to Enkidu belongs the episode with the woman, used to illustrate the evolution of primitive man to the ways and conditions of civilized life, the conquest of Ḫuwawa in the land of Amurru, the killing of lions and also of the bull, while Gilgamesh is the hero who conquers Erech. Identified with the sun-god, the nature myth of the union of the sun with the earth and the subsequent separation of the two is also transferred to him. The wanderings of the hero, smitten with disease, are a continuation of the nature myth, symbolizing the waning vigor of the sun with the approach of the wintry season.

The details of the process which led to making Gilgamesh the favorite figure, to whom the traits and exploits of Enkidu and of the sun-god are transferred, escape us, but of the fact that Enkidu is the *older* figure, of whom certain adventures were set forth in a tale that once had an independent existence, there can now be little doubt in the face of the evidence furnished by the two tablets of the old Babylonian version; just as the study of these tablets shows that in the combination of the tales of Enkidu and Gilgamesh, the former is the prototype of which Gilgamesh is the copy. If the two are regarded as brothers, as born in the same place, even resembling one another in appearance and carrying out their adventures in common, it is because in the process of combination Gilgamesh becomes the *reflex* of Enkidu. That Enkidu is not the figure created by Aruru to relieve Erech of its tyrannical ruler is also shown by the fact that Gilgamesh remains in control of Erech. It is to Erech that he returns when he fails of his purpose to learn the secret of escape from old age and death. Erech is, therefore, not relieved of the presence of the ruthless ruler through Enkidu. The

"Man of Anu" formed by Aruru as a deliverer is confused in the course of the growth of the Epic with Enkidu, the offspring of Ninib, and in this way we obtain the strange contradiction of Enkidu and Gilgamesh appearing first as bitter rivals and then as close and inseparable friends. It is of the nature of Epic compositions everywhere to eliminate unnecessary figures by concentrating on one favorite the traits belonging to another or to several others.

The close association of Enkidu and Gilgamesh which becomes one of the striking features in the combination of the tales of these two heroes naturally recalls the "Heavenly Twins" *motif*, which has been so fully and so suggestively treated by Professor J. Rendell Harris in his *Cult of the Heavenly Twins*, (London, 1906). Professor Harris has conclusively shown how widespread the tendency is to associate two divine or semi-divine beings in myths and legends as inseparable companions125 or twins, like Castor and Pollux, Romulus and Remus,126 the Acvins in the Rig-Veda,127 Cain and Abel, Jacob and Esau in the Old Testament, the Kabiri of the Phoenicians,128 Herakles and Iphikles in Greek mythology, Ambrica and Fidelio in Teutonic mythology, Patollo and Potrimpo in old Prussian mythology, Cautes and Cautopates in Mithraism, Jesus and Thomas (according to the Syriac Acts of Thomas), and the various illustrations of "Dioscuri in Christian Legends," set forth by Dr. Harris in his work under this title, which carries the *motif* far down into the period of legends about Christian Saints who appear in pairs, including the reference to such a pair in Shakespeare's Henry V:

"And Crispin Crispian shall ne'er go by

From that day to the ending of the world."—(*Act, IV, 3, 57–58.*)

There are indeed certain parallels which suggest that Enkidu-Gilgamesh may represent a Babylonian counterpart to the "Heavenly Twins." In the Indo-Iranian, Greek and Roman mythology, the twins almost invariably act together. In unison they proceed on expeditions to punish enemies.129

But after all, the parallels are of too general a character to be of much moment; and moreover the parallels stop short at the critical point, for Gilgamesh though worsted is *not* killed by Enkidu, whereas one of the "Heavenly Twins" is always killed by the brother, as Abel is by Cain, and Iphikles by his twin brother Herakles. Even the trait which is frequent in the earliest forms of the "Heavenly Twins," according to which one is immortal and the other is mortal, though applying in a measure to Enkidu who is killed by Ishtar, while Gilgamesh the offspring of a divine pair is only smitten with disease, is too unsubstantial to warrant more than a general comparison between the Enkidu-Gilgamesh pair and the various forms of the "twin" *motif* found throughout the ancient world. For all that, the point is of some interest that in the Gilgamesh Epic we should encounter two figures who are portrayed as possessing the same traits and accomplishing feats in common, which suggest a partial parallel to the various forms in which the twin-*motif* appears in the mythologies, folk-lore and legends of many nations; and it may be that in some of these instances the duplication is due, as in the case of Enkidu and Gilgamesh, to an actual transfer of the traits of one figure to another who usurped his place.

In concluding this study of the two recently discovered tablets of the old Babylonian version of the Gilgamesh Epic which has brought us several steps further in the interpretation and in our understanding of the method of composition of the most notable literary production of ancient Babylonia, it will be proper to consider the *literary* relationship of the old Babylonian to the Assyrian version.

We have already referred to the different form in which the names of the chief figures appear in the old Babylonian version, ^{d}Gish as against ^{d}Gish-gì(n)-mash, ^{d}En-ki-dũ as against ^{d}En-ki-dú, Ḫu-wa-wa as against Ḫu(m)-ba-ba. Erech appears as *Uruk ribîtim*, "Erech of the Plazas," as against *Uruk supûri*, "walled Erech" (or "Erech within the walls"), in the Assyrian version.130 These variations point to an *independent* recension for the Assyrian revision; and this conclusion is confirmed by a comparison of parallel passages in our two tablets with the Assyrian version, for such parallels rarely extend to verbal agreements in details, and, moreover, show that the Assyrian version has been elaborated.

Beginning with the Pennsylvania tablet, column I is covered in the Assyrian version by tablet I, 5, 25, to 6, 33, though, as pointed out above, in the Assyrian version we have the anticipation of the dreams of Gilgamesh and their interpretation through their recital to Enkidu by his female companion, whereas in the old Babylonian version we have the dreams *directly* given in a conversation between Gilgamesh and his mother. In the anticipation, there would naturally be some omissions. So lines 4–5 and 12–13 of the Pennsylvania tablet do not appear in the Assyrian version, but in their place is a line (I, 5, 35), to be restored to

"[I saw him and like] a woman I fell in love with him."

which occurs in the old Babylonian version only in connection with the second dream. The point is of importance as showing that in the Babylonian version the first dream lays stress upon the omen of the falling meteor, as symbolizing the coming of Enkidu, whereas the second dream more specifically reveals Enkidu as a man,131 of whom Gilgamesh is instantly enamored. Strikingly variant lines, though conveying the same idea, are frequent. Thus line 14 of the Babylonian version reads

"I bore it and carried it to thee"

and appears in the Assyrian version (I, 5, 35^b supplied from 6, 26)

"I threw it (or him) at thy feet"132

with an additional line in elaboration

"Thou didst bring him into contact with me"133

which anticipates the speech of the mother

(Line 41 = Assyrian version I, 6, 33).

Line 10 of the Pennsylvania tablet has *pa-ḫi-ir* as against *iz-za-az* I, 5, 31.

Line 8 has *ik-ta-bi-it* as against *da-an* in the Assyrian version I, 5, 29.

More significant is the variant to line 9

"I became weak and its weight I could not bear"

as against I, 5, 30.

"Its strength was overpowering,134 and I could not endure its weight."

The important lines 31–36 are not found in the Assyrian version, with the exception of I, 6, 27, which corresponds to lines 33–34, but this lack of correspondence is probably due to the fact that the Assyrian version represents the anticipation of the dreams which, as already suggested, might well omit some details. As against this we have in the

Assyrian version I, 6, 23–25, an elaboration of line 30 in the Pennsylvania tablet and taken over from the recital of the first dream. Through the Assyrian version I, 6, 31–32, we can restore the closing lines of column I of the Pennsylvania tablet, while with line 33 = line 45 of the Pennsylvania tablet, the parallel between the two versions comes to an end. Lines 34–43 of the Assyrian version (bringing tablet I to a close)135 represent an elaboration of the speech of Ninsun, followed by a further address of Gilgamesh to his mother, and by the determination of Gilgamesh to seek out Enkidu.136 Nothing of this sort appears to have been included in the old Babylonian version.Our text proceeds with the scene between Enkidu and the woman, in which the latter by her charms and her appeal endeavors to lead Enkidu away from his life with the animals. From the abrupt manner in which the scene is introduced in line 43 of the Pennsylvania tablet, it is evident that this cannot be the *first* mention of the woman. The meeting must have been recounted in the first tablet, as is the case in the Assyrian version.137 The second tablet takes up the direct recital of the dreams of Gilgamesh and then continues the narrative. Whether in the old Babylonian version the scene between Enkidu and the woman was described with the same naïve details, as in the Assyrian version, of the sexual intercourse between the two for six days and seven nights cannot of course be determined, though presumably the Assyrian version, with the tendency of epics to become more elaborate as they pass from age to age, added some realistic touches. Assuming that lines 44–63 of the Pennsylvania tablet—the cohabitation of Enkidu and the address of the woman—is a repetition of what was already described in the first tablet, the comparison with the Assyrian version I, 4, 16–41, not only points to the elaboration of the later version, but likewise to an independent recension, even where parallel lines can be picked out. Only lines 46–48 of the Pennsylvania tablet form a complete parallel to line 21 of column 4 of the Assyrian version. The description in lines 22–32 of column 4 is missing, though it may, of course, have been included in part in the recital in the first tablet of the old Babylonian version. Lines 49–59 of the Pennsylvania tablet are covered by 33–39, the only slight difference being the specific mention in line 58 of the Pennsylvania tablet of Eanna, the temple in Erech, described as "the dwelling of Anu," whereas in the Assyrian version Eanna is merely referred to as the "holy house" and described as "the dwelling of Anu and Ishtar," where Ishtar is clearly a later addition.

Leaving aside lines 60–61, which may be merely a variant (though independent) of line 39 of column 4 of the Assyrian version, we now have in the Pennsylvania tablet a second speech of the woman to Enkidu (not represented in the Assyrian version) beginning like the first one with *alka*, "Come" (lines 62–63), in which she asks Enkidu to leave the "accursed ground" in which he dwells. This speech, as the description which follows, extending into columns 3–4, and telling how the woman clothed Enkidu, how she brought him to the sheep folds, how she taught him to eat bread and to drink wine, and how she instructed him in the ways of civilization, must have been included in the second tablet of the Assyrian version which has come down to us in a very imperfect form. Nor is the scene in which Enkidu and Gilgamesh have their encounter found in the preserved portions of the second (or possibly the third) tablet of the Assyrian version, but only a brief reference to it in the fourth tablet,138 in which in Epic style the story is repeated, leading up to the second exploit—the joint campaign of Enkidu and Gilgamesh against Ḫuwawa. This reference, covering only seven lines, corresponds to lines 192–231 of the Pennsylvania tablet; but the former being the repetition and the latter the original recital, the comparison to be instituted merely reveals again the independence of the Assyrian version, as shown in the use of *kibsu*, "tread" (IV, 2, 46), for *šêpu*, "foot" (l. 216), *i-na-uš*, "quake" (line 5C), as against *ir-tu-tu* (ll. 221 and 226).

Such variants as

dGish êribam ûl iddin (l. 217)

against

dGilgamesh ana šurûbi ûl namdin, (IV, 2, 47).

and again

iṢṢabtûma kima lîm "they grappled at the gate of the family house" (IV, 2, 48),

against

iṢṢabtûma ina bâb bît emuti, "they grappled at the gate of the family house" (IV, 2, 48),

all point once more to the literary independence of the Assyrian version. The end of the conflict and the reconciliation of the two heroes is likewise missing in the Assyrian version. It may have been referred to at the beginning of column 3[139] of Tablet IV.

Coming to the Yale tablet, the few passages in which a comparison may be instituted with the fourth tablet of the Assyrian version, to which in a general way it must correspond, are not sufficient to warrant any conclusions, beyond the confirmation of the literary independence of the Assyrian version. The section comprised within lines 72–89, where Enkidu's grief at his friend's decision to fight Ḫuwawa is described[140], and he makes confession of his own physical exhaustion, *may* correspond to Tablet IV, column 4, of the Assyrian version. This would fit in with the beginning of the reverse, the first two lines of which (136–137) correspond to column 5 of the fourth tablet of the Assyrian version, with a variation "seven-fold fear"[141] as against "fear of men" in the Assyrian version. If lines 138–139 (in column 4) of the Yale tablet correspond to line 7 of column 5 of Tablet IV of the Assyrian version, we would again have an illustration of the elaboration of the later version by the addition of lines 3–6. But beyond this we have merely the comparison of the description of Ḫuwawa

"Whose roar is a flood, whose mouth is fire, and whose breath is death"

which occurs twice in the Yale tablet (lines 110–111 and 196–197), with the same phrase in the Assyrian version Tablet IV, 5, 3—but here, as just pointed out, with an elaboration.

Practically, therefore, the entire Yale tablet represents an addition to our knowledge of the Ḫuwawa episode, and until we are fortunate enough to discover more fragments of the fourth tablet of the Assyrian version, we must content ourselves with the conclusions reached from a comparison of the Pennsylvania tablet with the parallels in the Assyrian version.

It may be noted as a general point of resemblance in the exterior form of the old Babylonian and Assyrian versions that both were inscribed on tablets containing six columns, three on the obverse and three on the reverse; and that the length of the tablets—an average of 40 to 50 lines—was about the same, thus revealing in the external form a conventiona1 size for the tablets in the older period, which was carried over into later times.

1 See for further details of this royal library, Jastrow, *Civilization of Babylonia and Assyria*, p. 21 *seq*.

2 *Das Babylonische Nimrodepos* (Leipzig, 1884–1891), supplemented by Haupt's article *Die Zwölfte Tafel des Babylonischen Nimrodepos* in *BA* I, pp. 48–79, containing the fragments of the twelfth tablet. The fragments of the Epic in Ashurbanapal's library—some sixty—represent portions of several copies. Sin-liḳî-unnini—perhaps from Erech, since this name appears as that of a family in tablets from Erech (see Clay, *Legal Documents from Erech*, Index, p. 73)—is named in a list of texts (K 9717—Haupt's edition No. 51, line 18) as the editor of the Epic, though probably he was not the only compiler. Since the publication of Haupt's edition, a few fragments were added by him as an appendix to Alfred Jeremias *Izdubar-Nimrod* (Leipzig, 1891) Plates II–IV, and two more are embodied in Jensen's transliteration of all the fragments in the *Keilinschriftliche Bibliothek* VI; pp. 116–265, with elaborate notes, pp. 421–531. Furthermore a fragment, obtained from supplementary excavations at Kouyunjik, has been published by L. W. King in his *Supplement to the Catalogue of the Cuneiform Tablets in the Kouyunjik Collection of the British Cuneiform Tablets in the Kouyunjik Collection of the British Museum* No. 56 and *PSBA* Vol. 36, pp. 64–68. Recently a fragment of the 6th tablet from the excavations at Assur has been published by Ebeling, *Keilschrifttexte aus Assur Religiösen Inhalts* No. 115, and one may expect further portions to turn up.

The designation "Nimrod Epic" on the supposition that the hero of the Babylonian Epic is identical with Nimrod, the "mighty hunter" of Genesis 10, has now been generally abandoned, in the absence of any evidence that the Babylonian hero bore a name like Nimrod. For all that, the description of Nimrod as the "mighty hunter" and the occurrence of a "hunter" in the Babylonian Epic (Assyrian version Tablet I)—though he is not the hero—points to a confusion in the Hebrew form of the borrowed tradition between Gilgamesh and Nimrod. The latest French translation of the Epic is by Dhorme, *Choix de Textes Religieux Assyro-Babyloniens* (Paris, 1907), pp. 182–325; the latest German translation by Ungnad-Gressmann, *Das Gilgamesch-Epos* (Göttingen, 1911), with a valuable analysis and discussion. These two translations now supersede Jensen's translation in the *Keilinschriftliche Bibliothek*, which, however, is still valuable because of the detailed notes, containing a wealth of lexicographical material. Ungnad also gave a partial translation in Gressmann-Ranke, *Altorientalische Texte and Bilder* I, pp. 39–61. In English, we have translations of substantial portions by Muss-Arnolt in Harper's *Assyrian and Babylonian Literature* (New York, 1901), pp. 324–368; by Jastrow, *Religion of Babylonia and Assyria* (Boston, 1898), Chap. XXIII; by Clay in *Light on the Old Testament from Babel*, pp. 78–84; by Rogers in *Cuneiform Parallels to the Old Testament*, pp. 80–103; and most recently by Jastrow in *Sacred Books and Early Literature of the East* (ed. C. F. Horne, New York, 1917), Vol. I, pp. 187–220.

3 See Luckenbill in *JAOS*, Vol. 37, p. 452 *seq*. Prof. Clay, it should be added, clings to the older reading, Hammurabi, which is retained in this volume.

4 *ZA*, Vol. 14, pp. 277–292.

5 The survivor of the Deluge is usually designated as Ut-napishtim in the Epic, but in one passage (Assyrian version, Tablet XI, 196), he is designated as Atra-ḫasis "the very wise one." Similarly, in a second version of the Deluge story, also found in Ashurbanapal's library (IV R^2 additions, p. 9, line 11). The two names clearly point to two versions, which in accordance with the manner of ancient compositions were merged into one. See an article by Jastrow in *ZA*, Vol. 13, pp. 288–301.

6 Published by Scheil in *Recueil des Travaux*, etc. Vol. 20, pp. 55–58.

7 The text does not form part of the Gilgamesh Epic, as the colophon, differing from the one attached to the Epic, shows.

8 *Ein altbabylonisches Fragment des Gilgamosepos* (*MVAG* 1902, No. 1).

9 On these variant forms of the two names see the discussion below, p. 24.

10 The passage is paralleled by Ecc. 9, 7–9. See Jastrow, *A Gentle Cynic*, p. 172 *seq*.

11 Among the Nippur tablets in the collection of the University of Pennsylvania Museum. The fragment was published by Dr. Poebel in his *Historical and Grammatical Texts* No. 23. See also Poebel in the *Museum Journal*, Vol. IV, p. 47, and an article by Dr. Langdon in the

same Journal, Vol. VII, pp. 178–181, though Langdon fails to credit Dr. Poebel with the discovery and publication of the important tablet.

12 No. 55 in Langdon's *Historical and Religious Texts from the Temple Library of Nippur* (Munich, 1914).

13 No. 5 in his *Sumerian Liturgical Texts.* (Philadelphia, 1917)

14 See on this name below, p. 23.

15 See further below, p. 37 *seq.*

16 See Poebel, *Historical and Grammatical Texts*, No. 1, and Jastrow in *JAOS*, Vol. 36, pp. 122–131 and 274–299.

17 See an article by Jastrow, *Sumerian and Akkadian Views of Beginnings* (*JAOS* Vol. 36, pp. 274–299).

18 See on this point Eduard Meyer, *Sumerier und Semiten in Babylonien* (Berlin, 1906), p. 107 *seq.*, whose view is followed in Jastrow, *Civilization of Babylonia and Assyria*, p. 121. See also Clay, *Empire of the Amorites* (Yale University Press, 1919), p. 23 *et seq.*

19 See the discussion below, p. 24 *seq.*

20 Dr. Poebel published an article on the tablet in *OLZ*, 1914, pp. 4–6, in which he called attention to the correct name for the mother of Gilgamesh, which was settled by the tablet as Ninsun.

21 *Historical Texts* No. 2, Column 2, 26. See the discussion in *Historical and Grammatical Texts*, p. 123, *seq.*

22 See Fostat in *OLZ*, 1915, p. 367.

23 *Publications of the University of Pennsylvania Museum, Babylonian Section*, Vol. X, No. 3 (Philadelphia, 1917). It is to be regretted that Dr. Langdon should not have given full credit to Dr. Poebel for his discovery of the tablet. He merely refers in an obscure footnote to Dr. Poebel's having made a copy.

24 E.g., in the very first note on page 211, and again in a note on page 213.

25 Dr. Langdon neglected to copy the signs *4 šú-si* = 240 which appear on the edge of the tablet. He also misunderstood the word *šú-tu-ur* in the colophon which he translated "written," taking the word from a stem *šaṭâru*, "write." The form *šú-tu-ur* is III, 1, from *atâru*, "to be in

excess of," and indicates, presumably, that the text is a copy "enlarged" from an older original. See the Commentary to the colophon, p. 86.

26 *Museum Journal*, Vol. VIII, p. 29.

27 See below, p. 23.

28 I follow the enumeration of tablets, columns and lines in Jensen's edition, though some fragments appear to have been placed by him in a wrong position.

29 According to Bezold's investigation, *Verbalsuffixformen als Alterskriterien babylonisch-assyrischer Inschriften* (Heidelberg Akad. d. Wiss., Philos.-Histor. Klasse, 1910, 9te Abhandlung), the bulk of the tablets in Ashurbanapal's library are copies of originals dating from about 1500 B.C. It does not follow, however, that all the copies date from originals of the same period. Bezold reaches the conclusion on the basis of various forms for verbal suffixes, that the fragments from the Ashurbanapal Library actually date from three distinct periods ranging from before c. 1450 to c. 700 B.C.

30 "Before thou comest from the mountain, Gilgamesh in Erech will see thy dreams," after which the dreams are recounted by the woman to Enkidu. The expression "thy dreams" means here "dreams about thee." (Tablet I, 5, 23–24).

31 Lines 100–101.

32 In a paper read before the American Oriental Society at New Haven, April 4, 1918.

33 See the commentary to col. 4 of the Yale tablet for further details.

34 This is no doubt the correct reading of the three signs which used to be read Iz-tu-bar or Gish-du-bar. The first sign has commonly the value Gish, the second can be read Gin or Gi (Brünnow No. 11900) and the third Mash as well as Bar. See Ungnad in Ungnad-Gressmann, *Das Gilgamesch-Epos*, p. 76, and Poebel, *Historical and Grammatical Texts*, p. 123.

35 So also in Sumerian (Zimmern, *Sumerische Kultlieder aus altbabylonischer Zeit*, No. 196, rev. 14 and 16.)

36 The sign used, LUM (Brünnow No. 11183), could have the value ḫu as well as ḫum.

37 The addition "father-in-law of Moses" to the name Ḫobab b. Re'uel in this passage must refer to Re'uel, and not to Ḫobab. In Judges 4, 11, the gloss "of the Bene Ḫobab, the father-in-law of Moses" must be separated into two: (1) "Bene Ḫobab," and (2) "father-in-law of Moses." The latter addition rests on an erroneous tradition, or is intended as a brief reminder that Ḫobab is identical with the son of Re'uel.

38 See his *List of Personal Names from the Temple School of Nippur*, p. 122. *Ḫu-um-ba-bi-tu* and *ši-kin ḫu-wa-wa* also occur in Omen Texts (*CT* XXVII, 4, 8–9 = Pl. 3, 17 = Pl. 6, 3–4 = *CT* XXVIII, 14, 12). The contrast to *ḫuwawa* is *ligru*, "dwarf" (*CT* XXVII, 4, 12 and 14 = Pl. 6, 7.9 = Pl. 3, 19). See Jastrow, *Religion Babyloniens und Assyriens*, II, p. 913, Note 7. Ḫuwawa, therefore, has the force of "monster."

39 Ungnad-Gressmann, *Das Gilgamesch-Epos*, p. 111 *seq.*

40 Ungnad, 1. c. p. 77, called attention to this name, but failed to draw the conclusion that Ḫu(m)baba therefore belongs to the West and not to the East.

41 First pointed out by Ungnad in *OLZ* 1910, p. 306, on the basis of *CT* XVIII, 30, 10, where En-gi-dú appears in the column furnishing *phonetic* readings.

42 See Clay *Amurru*, pp. 74, 129, etc.

43 Tablet I, 2, 39–40; 3, 6–7 and 33–34; 4, 3–4.

44 Tablet I, 2, 1 and IX, 2, 16. Note also the statement about Gilgamesh that "his body is flesh of the gods" (Tablet IX, 2, 14; X, 1, 7).

45 *BOR* IV, p. 264.

46 Lewin, *Die Scholien des Theodor bar Koni zur Patriarchengeschichte* (Berlin, 1905), p. 2. See Gressmann in Ungnad-Gressmann, *Das Gilgamesch-Epos*, p. 83, who points out that the first element of גלמגוס compared with the second of גמיגמוס gives the exact form that we require, namely, Gilgamos.

47 Tablet I, col. 2, is taken up with this episode.

48 See Poebel, *Historical and Grammatical Texts*, p. 123.

49 See Poebel, *Historical Texts* No. 2, col. 2, 26.

50 Hilprecht, *Old Babylonian Inscriptions* I, 1 No. 26.

51 Delitzsch, *Assyrische Lesestücke*, p. 88, VI, 2–3. Cf. also *CT* XXV, 28(K 7659) 3, where we must evidently supply [Esigga]-tuk, for which in the following line we have again Gish-bil-ga-mesh as an equivalent. See Meissner, *OLZ* 1910, 99.

52 See, e.g., Barton, *Haverford Collection* II No. 27, Col. I, 14, etc.

53 Deimel, *Pantheon Babylonicum*, p. 95.

54 *CT* XII, 50 (K 4359) obv. 17.

55 See Barton, *Origin and Development of Babylonian Writing*, II, p. 99 *seq*., for various explanations, though all centering around the same idea of the picture of fire in some form.

56 See the passages quoted by Poebel, *Historical and Grammatical Texts*, p. 126.

57 E.g., Genesis 4, 20, Jabal, "the father of tent-dwelling and cattle holding;" Jubal (4, 21), "the father of harp and pipe striking."

58 See particularly the plays (in the J. Document) upon the names of the twelve sons of Jacob, which are brought forward either as tribal characteristics, or as suggested by some incident or utterance by the mother at the birth of each son.

59 The designation is variously explained by Arabic writers. See Beidhawi's *Commentary* (ed. Fleischer), to Súra 18, 82.

60 The writing Gish-gi-mash as an approach to the pronunciation Gilgamesh would thus represent the beginning of the artificial process which seeks to interpret the first syllable as "hero."

61 See above, p. 27.

62 Poebel, *Historical Texts*, p. 115 *seq*.

63 Many years ago (*BA* III, p. 376) I equated Etana with Ethan in the Old Testament—therefore a West Semitic name.

64 See Clay, *The Empire of the Amorites*, p. 80.

65 Professor Clay strongly favors an Amoritic origin also for Gilgamesh. His explanation of the name is set forth in his recent work

on *The Empire of the Amorites*, page 89, and is also referred to in his work on *Amurru*, page 79, and in his volume of *Miscellaneous Inscriptions in the Yale Babylonian Collection*, page 3, note. According to Professor Clay the original form of the hero's name was West Semitic, and was something like *Bilga-Mash*, the meaning of which was perhaps "the offspring of Mash." For the first element in this division of the name cf. Piliḳam, the name of a ruler of an early dynasty, and Balaḳ of the Old Testament. In view of the fact that the axe figures so prominently in the Epic as an instrument wielded by Gilgamesh, Professor Clay furthermore thinks it reasonable to assume that the name was interpreted by the Babylonian scribe as "the axe of Mash." In this way he would account for the use of the determinative for weapons, which is also the sign Gish, in the name. It is certainly noteworthy that the ideogram Gish-Tún in the later form of *Gish-Tún-mash* = *pašu*, "axe," *CT* XVI, 38:14b, etc. *Tun* also = *pilaḳu* "axe," *CT* xii, 10:34b. Names with similar element (besides Piliḳam) are Belaḳu of the Hammurabi period, Bilaḳḳu of the Cassite period, etc.

It is only proper to add that Professor Jastrow assumes the responsibility for the explanation of the form and etymology of the name Gilgamesh proposed in this volume. The question is one in regard to which legitimate differences of opinion will prevail among scholars until through some chance a definite decision, one way or the other, can be reached.

66 *me-iḫ-rù* (line 191).

67 Tablet I, 5, 23. Cf. I, 3, 2 and 29.

68 Tablet IV, 4, 7 and I, 5, 3.

69 Assyrian version, Tablet II, 3b 34, in an address of Shamash to Enkidu.

70 So Assyrian version, Tablet VIII, 3, 11. Also supplied VIII, 5, 20 and 21; and X, 1, 46–47 and 5, 6–7.

71 Tablet XII, 3, 25.

72 Ward, *Seal Cylinders of Western Asia*, Chap. X, and the same author's *Cylinders and other Ancient Oriental Seals*—Morgan collection Nos. 19–50.

73 E.g., Ward No. 192, Enkidu has human legs like Gilgamesh; also No. 189, where it is difficult to say which is Gilgamesh, and which is

Enkidu. The clothed one is probably Gilgamesh, though not infrequently Gilgamesh is also represented as nude, or merely with a girdle around his waist.

74 E.g., Ward, Nos. 173, 174, 190, 191, 195 as well as 189 and 192.

75 On the other hand, in Ward Nos. 459 and 461, the conflict between the two heroes is depicted with the heroes distinguished in more conventional fashion, Enkidu having the hoofs of an animal, and also with a varying arrangement of beard and hair.

76 See Jastrow, *Religion of Babylonia and Assyria* (Boston, 1898), p. 468 *seq.*

77 Ungnad-Gressmann, *Das Gilgamesch-Epos*, p. 90 *seq.*

78 Pennsylvania tablet, l. 198 = Assyrian version, Tablet IV, 2, 37.

79 "Enkidu blocked the gate" (Pennsylvania tablet, line 215) = Assyrian version Tablet IV, 2, 46: "Enkidu interposed his foot at the gate of the family house."

80 Pennsylvania tablet, lines 218 and 224.

81 Yale tablet, line 198; also to be supplied lines 13–14.

82 Yale tablet, lines 190 and 191.

83 *PSBA* 1914, 65 *seq.* = Jensen III, 1[a], 4–11, which can now be completed and supplemented by the new fragment.

84 I.e., Enkidu will save Gilgamesh.

85 These two lines impress one as popular sayings—here applied to Enkidu.

86 King's fragment, col. I, 13–27, which now enables us to complete Jensen III, 1[a], 12–21.

87 Yale tablet, lines 252–253.

88 Yale tablet, lines 143–148 = Assyrian version, Tablet IV, 6, 26 *seq.*

89 Assyrian version, Tablet III, 2[a], 13–14.

90 Lines 215–222.

91 Assyrian version, Tablet V, Columns 3–4. We have to assume that in line 13 of column 4 (Jensen, p. 164), Enkidu takes up the thread of

conversation, as is shown by line 22: "Enkidu brought his dream to him and spoke to Gilgamesh."

92 Assyrian version, Tablet VI, lines 146–147.

93 Lines 178–183.

94 Lines 176–177.

95 Tablet VII, Column 6.

96 Assyrian version, Tablet VI, 200–203. These words are put into the mouth of Gilgamesh (lines 198–199). It is, therefore, unlikely that he would sing his own praise. Both Jensen and Ungnad admit that Enkidu is to be supplied in at least one of the lines.

97 Lines 109 and 112.

98 Assyrian version, Tablet IX, 1, 8–9.

99 Tablet VIII, 5, 2–6.

100 So also Gressmann in Ungnad-Gressmann, *Das Gilgamesch-Epos*, p. 97, regards Enkidu as the older figure.

101 See Jastrow, *Adam and Eve in Babylonian Literature, AJSL*, Vol. 15, pp. 193–214.

102 Assyrian version, Tablet I, 2, 31–36.

103 It will be recalled that Enkidu is always spoken of as "born in the field."

104 Note the repetition *ibtani* "created" in line 33 of the "man of Anu" and in line 35 of the offspring of Ninib. The creation of the former is by the "heart," i.e., by the will of Aruru, the creation of the latter is an act of moulding out of clay.

105 Tablet I, Column 3.

106 Following as usual the enumeration of lines in Jensen's edition.

107 An analogy does not involve a dependence of one tale upon the other, but merely that both rest on similar traditions, which *may* have arisen independently.

108 Note that the name of Eve is not mentioned till after the fall (Genesis 3, 20). Before that she is merely *ishsha*, i.e., "woman," just as

in the Babylonian tale the woman who guides Enkidu is *ḫarimtu*, "woman."

109 "And he drank and became drunk" (Genesis 9, 21).

110 "His heart became glad and his face shone" (Pennsylvania Tablet, lines 100–101).

111 That in the combination of this Enkidu with tales of primitive man, inconsistent features should have been introduced, such as the union of Enkidu with the woman as the beginning of a higher life, whereas the presence of a hunter and his father shows that human society was already in existence, is characteristic of folk-tales, which are indifferent to details that may be contradictory to the general setting of the story.

112 Pennsylvania tablet, lines 102–104.

113 Line 105.

114 Tablet I, 1, 9. See also the reference to the wall of Erech as an "old construction" of Gilgamesh, in the inscription of An-Am in the days of Sin-gamil (Hilprecht, *Old Babylonian Inscriptions*, I, No. 26.) Cf IV R^2 52, 3, 53.

115 The invariable designation in the Assyrian version as against *Uruk ribîtim*, "Erech of the plazas," in the old Babylonian version.

116 In Ungnad-Gressmann, *Das Gilgamesch-Epos*, p. 123 *seq.*

117 See Jensen, p. 266. Gilgamesh is addressed as "judge," as the one who inspects the divisions of the earth, precisely as Shamash is celebrated. In line 8 of the hymn in question, Gilgamesh is in fact addressed as Shamash.

118 The darkness is emphasized with each advance in the hero's wanderings (Tablet IX, col. 5).

119 This tale is again a nature myth, marking the change from the dry to the rainy season. The Deluge is an annual occurrence in the Euphrates Valley through the overflow of the two rivers. Only the canal system, directing the overflow into the fields, changed the curse into a blessing. In contrast to the Deluge, we have in the Assyrian creation story the drying up of the primeval waters so that the earth makes its appearance with the change from the rainy to the dry season.

The world is created in the spring, according to the Akkadian view which is reflected in the Biblical creation story, as related in the P. document. See Jastrow, *Sumerian and Akkadian Views of Beginnings* (*JAOS*, Vol 36, p. 295 seq.).

120 Aš-am in Sumerian corresponding to the Akkadian Šabaṭu, which conveys the idea of destruction.

121 The month is known as the "Mission of Ishtar" in Sumerian, in allusion to another nature myth which describes Ishtar's disappearance from earth and her mission to the lower world.

122 *Historical Texts* No. 1. The Sumerian name of the survivor is Zi-ū-gíd-du or perhaps Zi-ū-sū-du (cf. King, *Legends of Babylon and Egypt*, p. 65, note 4), signifying "He who lengthened the day of life," i.e., the one of long life, of which Ut-napishtim ("Day of Life") in the Assyrian version seems to be an abbreviated Akkadian rendering, with the omission of the verb. So King's view, which is here followed. See also *CT* XVIII, 30, 9, and Langdon, *Sumerian Epic of Paradise*, p. 90, who, however, enters upon further speculations that are fanciful.

123 See the translation in Ungnad-Gressmann, *Das Gilgamesch-Epos*, pp. 69, *seq.* and 73.

124 According to Professor Clay, quite certainly Amurru, just as in the case of Enkidu.

125 Gressmann in Ungnad-Gressmann, *Das Gilgamesch-Epos*, p. 100 *seq.* touches upon this *motif*, but fails to see the main point that the companions are also twins or at least brothers. Hence such examples as Abraham and Lot, David and Jonathan, Achilles and Patroclus, Eteokles and Polyneikes, are not parallels to Gilgamesh-Enkidu, but belong to the *enlargement* of the *motif* so as to include companions who are *not* regarded as brothers.

126 Or Romus. See Rendell Harris, l. c., p. 59, note 2.

127 One might also include the primeval pair Yama-Yami with their equivalents in Iranian mythology (Carnoy, *Iranian Mythology*, p. 294 *seq.*).

128 Becoming, however, a triad and later increased to seven. Cf. Rendell Harris, l. c., p. 32.

129 I am indebted to my friend, Professor A. J. Carnoy, of the University of Louvain, for having kindly gathered and placed at my

disposal material on the "twin-brother" *motif* from Indo-European sources, supplemental to Rendell Harris' work.

130 On the other hand, *Uruk mâtum* for the district of Erech, i.e., the territory over which the city holds sway, appears in both versions (Pennsylvania tablet, 1. 10 = Assyrian version I, 5, 36).

131 "My likeness" (line 27). It should be noted, however, that lines 32–44 of I, 5, in Jensen's edition are part of a fragment K 9245 (not published, but merely copied by Bezold and Johns, and placed at Jensen's disposal), which may represent a *duplicate* to I, 6, 23–34, with which it agrees entirely except for one line, viz., line 34 of K 9245 which is not found in column 6, 23–34. If this be correct, then there is lacking after line 31 of column 5, the interpretation of the dream given in the Pennsylvania tablet in lines 17–23.

132 *ina šap-li-ki*, literally, "below thee," whereas in the old Babylonian version we have *ana Ṣi-ri-ka*, "towards thee."

133 Repeated I, 6, 28.

134 *ul-tap-rid ki-is-su-šú-ma*. The verb is from *parâdu*, "violent." For *kissu*, "strong," see *CT* XVI, 25, 48–49. Langdon (*Gilgamesh Epic*, p. 211, note 5) renders the phrase: "he shook his murderous weapon!!"—another illustration of his haphazard way of translating texts.

135 Shown by the colophon (Jeremias, *Izdubar-Nimrod*, Plate IV.)

136 Lines 42–43 must be taken as part of the narrative of the compiler, who tells us that after the woman had informed Enkidu that Gilgamesh already knew of Enkidu's coming through dreams interpreted by Ninsun, Gilgamesh actually set out and encountered Enkidu.

137 Tablet I, col. 4. See also above, p. 19.

138 IV, 2, 44–50. The word *ullanum*, (l.43) "once" or "since," points to the following being a reference to a former recital, and not an original recital.

139 Only the lower half (Haupt's edition, p. 82) is preserved.

140 "The eyes of Enkidu were filled with tears," corresponding to IV, 4, 10.

141 Unless indeed the number "seven" is a slip for the sign ša. See the commentary to the line.

Pennsylvania Tablet

The 240 lines of the six columns of the text are enumerated in succession, with an indication on the margin where a new column begins. This method, followed also in the case of the Yale tablet, seems preferable to Langdon's breaking up of the text into Obverse and Reverse, with a separate enumeration for each of the six columns. In order, however, to facilitate a comparison with Langdon's edition, a table is added:

Obverse Col.	I, 1	= Line	1 of our text.
"	I, 5	= "	5 " " "
"	I, 10	= "	10 " " "
"	I, 15	= "	15 " " "
"	I, 20	= "	20 " " "
"	I, 25	= "	25 " " "
"	I, 30	= "	30 " " "
"	I, 35	= "	35 " " "
Col.	II, 1	= Line	41 " " "
"	II, 5	= "	45 " " "
"	II, 10	= "	50 " " "
"	II, 15	= "	55 " " "
"	II, 20	= "	60 " " "
"	II, 25	= "	65 " " "
"	II, 30	= "	70 " " "
"	II, 35	= "	75 " " "
Col.	III, 1	= Line	81 " " "

,,	III, 5	= ,,	85 ,, ,, ,,
,,	III, 10	= ,,	90 ,, ,, ,,
,,	III, 15	= ,,	95 ,, ,, ,,
,,	III, 26	= ,,	100 ,, ,, ,,
,,	III, 25	= ,,	105 ,, ,, ,,
,,	III, 30	= ,,	110 ,, ,, ,,
,,	III, 35	= ,,	115 ,, ,, ,,
Reverse Col.	I, 1 (= Col. IV)	= Line	131 of our text.
,,	I, 5	= ,,	135 ,, ,, ,,
,,	I, 10	= ,,	140 ,, ,, ,,
,,	I, 15	= ,,	145 ,, ,, ,,
,,	I, 20	= ,,	150 ,, ,, ,,
,,	I, 25	= ,,	155 ,, ,, ,,
,,	I, 30	= ,,	160 ,, ,, ,,
,,	II, 1 (= Col. V)	= Line	171 ,, ,, ,,
,,	II, 5	= ,,	175 ,, ,, ,,
,,	II, 10	= ,,	180 ,, ,, ,,
,,	II, 15	= ,,	185 ,, ,, ,,
,,	II, 20	= ,,	190 ,, ,, ,,
,,	II, 25	= ,,	195 ,, ,, ,,
,,	II, 30	= ,,	200 ,, ,, ,,
,,	III, 1 (= Col. VI)	= Line	208 ,, ,, ,,
,,	III, 5	= ,,	212 ,, ,, ,,
,,	III, 10	= ,,	217 ,, ,, ,,
,,	III, 15	= ,,	222 ,, ,, ,,
,,	III, 20	= ,,	227 ,, ,, ,,
,,	III, 25	= ,,	232 ,, ,, ,,

„	III, 30	= „	237 „ „ „
„	III, 33	= „	240 „ „ „

Pennsylvania Tablet.

Transliteration.

Col. I.

1it-bi-e-ma ^{d}Giš šú-na-tam i-pa-áš-šar

2iz-za-kàr-am a-na um-mi-šú

3um-mi i-na šá-at mu-ši-ti-ia

4šá-am-ḫa-ku-ma at-ta-na-al-la-ak

5i-na bi-ri-it it-lu-tim

6ib-ba-šú-nim-ma ka-ka-bu šá-ma-i

7[ki]-iṣ-rù šá A-nim im-ḳu-ut a-na Ṣi-ri-ia

8áš-ši-šú-ma ik-ta-bi-it e-li-ia

9ú-ni-iš-šú-ma nu-uš-šá-šú ú-ul il-ti-'i

10Uruk^{ki} ma-tum pa-ḫi-ir e-li-šú

11it-lu-tum ú-na-šá-ku ši-pi-šú

12ú-um-mi-id-ma pu-ti

13i-mi-du ia-ti

14áš-ši-a-šú-ma ab-ba-la-áš-šú a-na Ṣi-ri-ki

15um-mi ^{d}Giš mu-di-a-at ka-la-ma

16iz-za-kàr-am a-na ^{d}Giš

17mi-in-di ^{d}Giš šá ki-ma ka-ti

18i-na Ṣi-ri i-wa-li-id-ma

19ú-ra-ab-bi-šú šá-du-ú

20ta-mar-šú-ma [kima Sal(?)] ta-ḫa-du at-ta

21it-lu-tum ú-na-šá-ku ši-pi-šú

22tí-iṭ-ṭi-ra-áš-[šú tu-ut]-tu-ú-ma

23ta-tar-ra-[as-su] a-na ṣi-[ri]-ia

24[uš]-ti-nim-ma i-ta-mar šá-ni-tam

25[šú-na]-ta i-ta-wa-a-am a-na um-mi-šú

26[um-mi] a-ta-mar šá-ni-tam

27[šú-na-tu a-ta]-mar e-mi-a i-na su-ḳi-im

28[šá Uruk]^{ki} ri-bi-tim

29ḫa-aṣ-ṣi-nu na-di-i-ma

30e-li-šú pa-aḫ-ru

31ḫa-aṣ-ṣi-nu-um-ma šá-ni bu-nu-šú

32a-mur-šú-ma aḫ-ta-du a-na-ku

33a-ra-am-šú-ma ki-ma áš-šá-tim

34a-ḫa-ab-bu-ub el-šú

35el-ki-šú-ma áš-ta-ka-an-šú

36a-na a-ḫi-ia

37um-mi ^{d}Giš mu-da-at [ka]-la-ma

38[iz-za-kàr-am a-na ^{d}Giš]

39[^{d}Giš šá ta-mu-ru amêlu]

40[ta-ḫa-ab-bu-ub ki-ma áš-šá-tim el-šú]

Col. II.

41áš-šum uš-[ta]-ma-ḫa-ru it-ti-ka

42^{d}Giš šú-na-tam i-pa-šar

43^{d}En-ki-[dũ wa]-ši-ib ma-ḫar ḫa-ri-im-tim

44ur-[šá ir]-ḫa-mu di-da-šá(?) ip-tí-[e]

45[^{d}En-ki]-dũ im-ta-ši a-šar i-wa-al-du

46ûm, 6 ù 7 mu-ši-a-tim

47^{d}En-[ki-dũ] ti-bi-i-ma

48šá-[am-ka-ta] ir-ḫi

49ḫa-[ri-im-tum pa-a]-šá i-pu-šá-am-ma

50iz-za-[kàr-am] a-na ^{d}En-ki-dũ

51a-na-tal-ka ^{d}En-ki-dũ ki-ma ili ta-ba-áš-ši

52am-mi-nim it-ti na-ma-áš-te-e

53ta-at-ta-[na-al]-ak ṣi-ra-am

54al-kam lu-úr-di-ka

55a-na libbi [Uruk^{ki}] ri-bi-tim

56a-na bît [el]-lim mu-šá-bi šá A-nim

57^{d}En-ki-dũ ti-bi lu-ru-ka

58a-na Ê-[an]-na mu-šá-bi šá A-nim

59a-šar [^{d}Giš gi]-it-ma-[lu] ne-pi-ši-tim

60ù at-[ta] ki-[ma Sal ta-ḫa]-bu-[ub]-šú

61ta-[ra-am-šú ki-ma] ra-ma-an-ka

62al-ka ti-ba i-[na] ga-ag-ga-ri

63ma-a-ag-ri-i-im

64iš-me a-wa-as-sa im-ta-ḫar ga-ba-šá

65mi-il-[kum] šá aššatim

66im-ta-ḳu-ut a-na libbi-šú

67iš-ḫu-ut li-ib-šá-am

68iš-ti-nam ú-la-ab-bi-iš-sú

69li-ib-[šá-am] šá-ni-a-am

70ši-i it-ta-al-ba-áš

71ṣa-ab-tat ga-as-su

72ki-ma [ili] i-ri-id-di-šú

73a-na gu-up-ri šá-ri-i-im

74a-šar tar-ba-Ṣi-im

75i-na [áš]-ri-šú [im]-ḫu-ruri-ia-ú

76[ù šú-u ^{d}En-ki-dũ i-lit-ta-šú šá-du-um-ma]

77[it-ti Ṣabâti-ma ik-ka-la šam-ma]

78[it-ti bu-lim maš-Ḳa-a i-šat-ti]

79[it-ti na-ma-áš-te-e mê i-Ṭab lib-ba-šú]

(Perhaps one additional line missing.)

Col. III.

81ši-iz-ba šá na-ma-áš-te-e

82i-te-en-ni-ik

83a-ka-lam iš-ku-nu ma-ḫar-šú

84ib-tí-ik-ma i-na-at-tal

85ù ip-pa-al-la-as

86ú-ul i-di ^{d}En-ki-dũ

87aklam a-na a-ka-lim

88šikaram a-na šá-te-e-im

89la-a lum-mu-ud

90ḫa-ri-im-tum pi-šá i-pu-šá-am-ma

91iz-za-kàr-am a-na ^{d}En-ki-dũ

92a-ku-ul ak-lam ^{d}En-ki-dũ

93zi-ma-at ba-la-Ṭi-im

94šikaram ši-ti ši-im-ti ma-ti

95i-ku-ul a-ak-lam ^{d}En-ki-dũ

96a-di ši-bi-e-šú

97šikaram iš-ti-a-am

987 aṢ-Ṣa-am-mi-im

99it-tap-šar kab-ta-tum i-na-an-gu

100i-li-iṣ libba-šú-ma

101pa-nu-šú [it]-tam-ru

102ul-tap-pi-it [^{lù}ŠÚ]-I

103šú-ḫu-ra-am pa-ga-ar-šú

104šá-am-nam ip-ta-šá-áš-ma

105a-we-li-iš i-we

106il-ba-áš li-ib-šá-am

107ki-ma mu-ti i-ba-áš-ši

108il-ki ka-ak-ka-šú

109la-bi ú-gi-ir-ri

110uš-sa-ak-pu re'ûti mu-ši-a-tim

111ut-tap-pi-iš šib-ba-ri

112la-bi uk-ta-ši-id

113it-ti-[lu] na-ki-[di-e] ra-bu-tum

114^{d}En-ki-dũ ma-aṣ-ṣa-ar-šú-nu

115a-we-lum giš-ru-um

116iš-te-en it-lum

117a-na [na-ki-di-e(?) i]-za-ak-ki-ir

(About five lines missing.)

Col. IV.

(About eight lines missing.)

131i-ip-pu-uš ul-ṣa-am

132iš-ši-ma i-ni-i-šú

133i-ta-mar a-we-lam

134iz-za-kàr-am a-na ḫarimtim

135šá-am-ka-at uk-ki-ši a-we-lam

136a-na mi-nim il-li-kam

137zi-ki-ir-šú lu-uš-šú

138ḫa-ri-im-tum iš-ta-si a-we-lam

139i-ba-uš-su-um-ma i-ta-mar-šú

140e-di-il e-eš ta-ḫi-[il-la]-am

141lim-nu a-la-ku ma-na-aḫ-[ti]-ka

142e-pi-šú i-pu-šá-am-ma

143iz-za-kàr-am a-na ^{d}En-[ki-dũ]

144bi-ti-iš e-mu-tim ik ......

145ši-ma-a-at ni-ši-i-ma

146tu-a-(?)-ar e-lu-tim

147a-na âli(?) dup-šak-ki-i e-ṣi-en

148uk-la-at âli(?) e-mi-sa a-a-ḫa-tim

149a-na šarri šá Uruk^{ki} ri-bi-tim

150pi-ti pu-uk epiši(-ši) a-na ḫa-a-a-ri

151a-na ^{d}Giš šarri šá Uruk^{ki} ri-bi-tim

152pi-ti pu-uk epiši(-ši)

153a-na ḫa-a-a-ri

154áš-ša-at ši-ma-tim i-ra-aḫ-ḫi

155šú-ú pa-na-nu-um-ma

156mu-uk wa-ar-ka-nu

157i-na mi-il-ki šá ili ga-bi-ma

158i-na bi-ti-iḳ a-bu-un-na-ti-šú

159ši-ma-as-su

160a-na zi-ik-ri it-li-im

161i-ri-ku pa-nu-šú

(About three lines missing.)

Col. V.

(About six lines missing.)

171i-il-la-ak [^{d}En-ki-dũ i-na pa-ni]

172u-šá-am-ka-at [wa]-ar-ki-šú

173i-ru-ub-ma a-na libbi Uruk^{ki} ri-bi-tim

174ip-ḫur um-ma-nu-um i-na Ṣi-ri-šú

175iz-zi-za-am-ma i-na su-ḳi-im

176šá Uruk^{ki} ri-bi-tim

177pa-aḫ-ra-a-ma ni-šú

178i-ta-wa-a i-na Ṣi-ri-šú

179a-na Ṣalam ^{d}Giš ma-ši-il pi-it-tam

180la-nam šá-pi-il

181si-ma .... [šá-ki-i pu]-uk-ku-ul

182............ i-pa-ka-du

183i-[na mâti da-an e-mu]-ki i-wa

184ši-iz-ba šá na-ma-aš-te-e

185i-te-en-ni-ik

186ka-a-a-na i-na [libbi] Uruk^{ki} kak-ki-a-tum

187it-lu-tum ú-te-el-li-lu

188šá-ki-in ur-šá-nu

189a-na itli šá i-šá-ru zi-mu-šú

190a-na ^{d}Giš ki-ma i-li-im

191šá-ki-iš-šum me-iḫ-rù

192a-na ^{d}Iš-ḫa-ra ma-a-a-lum

193na-di-i-ma

194^{d}Giš it-[ti-il-ma wa-ar-ka-tim]

195i-na mu-ši in-ni-[ib-bi]-it

196i-na-ag-šá-am-ma

197it-ta-[zi-iz dEn-ki-dũ] i-na sûḳim

198ip-ta-ra-[aṣ a-la]-ak-tam

199šá ^{d}Giš

200[a-na e-pi-iš] da-na-ni-iš-šú

(About three lines missing.)

Col. VI.

(About four lines missing.)

208šar(?)-ḫa

209^{d}Giš …

210i-na ṣi-ri-[šú il-li-ka-am ^{d}En-ki-dũ]

211i-ḫa-an-ni-ib [pi-ir-ta-šú]

212it-bi-ma [il-li-ik]

213a-na pa-ni-šú

214it-tam-ḫa-ru i-na ri-bi-tum ma-ti

215^{d}En-ki-dũ ba-ba-am ip-ta-ri-ik

216i-na ši-pi-šú

217^{d}Giš e-ri-ba-am ú-ul id-di-in

218iṣ-ṣa-ab-tu-ma ki-ma li-i-im

219i-lu-du

220zi-ip-pa-am ’i-bu-tu

221i-ga-rum ir-tu-tu

222^{d}Giš ù ^{d}En-ki-dũ

223iṣ-ṣa-ab-tu-ú-ma

224ki-ma li-i-im i-lu-du

225zi-ip-pa-am ’i-bu-tu

226i-ga-rum ir-tu-tú

227ik-mi-is-ma ^{d}Giš

228i-na ga-ag-ga-ri ši-ip-šú

229ip-ši-iḫ uz-za-šú-ma

230i-ni-iḫ i-ra-as-su

231iš-tu i-ra-su i-ni-ḫu

232^{d}En-ki-dũ a-na šá-ši-im

233iz-za-kàr-am a-na ^{d}Giš

234ki-ma iš-te-en-ma um-ma-ka

235ú-li-id-ka

236ri-im-tum šá su-pu-ri

237^{d}Nin-sun-na

238ul-lu e-li mu-ti ri-eš-ka

239šar-ru-tú šá ni-ši

240i-ši-im-kum ^{d}En-lil

241 duppu 2 kam-ma

242šú-tu-ur e-li …………………

243 4 šú-ši

Translation.

Col. I.

1Gish sought to interpret the dream;

2Spoke to his mother:

3"My mother, during my night

4I became strong and moved about

5among the heroes;

6And from the starry heaven

7A meteor(?) of Anu fell upon me:

8I bore it and it grew heavy upon me,

9I became weak and its weight I could not endure.

The land of Erech gathered about it.
The heroes kissed its feet.[1]
It was raised up before me.
They stood me up.[2]
I bore it and carried it to thee."
The mother of Gish, who knows all things,
Spoke to Gish:
"Some one, O Gish, who like thee
In the field was born and
Whom the mountain has reared,
Thou wilt see (him) and [like a woman(?)] thou wilt rejoice.
Heroes will kiss his feet.
Thou wilt spare [him and wilt endeavor]
To lead him to me."
He slept and saw another
Dream, which he reported to his mother:
["My mother,] I have seen another
[Dream.] My likeness I have seen in the streets
[Of Erech] of the plazas.
An axe was brandished, and
They gathered about him;
And the axe made him angry.
I saw him and I rejoiced,
I loved him as a woman,
I embraced him.
I took him and regarded him
As my brother."

37The mother of Gish, who knows all things,

38[Spoke to Gish]:

39[“O Gish, the man whom thou sawest,]

40[Whom thou didst embrace like a woman].

Col II.

41(means) that he is to be associated with thee.”

42Gish understood the dream.

43[As] Enki[du] was sitting before the woman,

44[Her] loins(?) he embraced, her vagina(?) he opened.

45[Enkidu] forgot the place where he was born.

46Six days and seven nights

47Enkidu continued

48To cohabit with [the courtesan].

49[The woman] opened her [mouth] and

50Spoke to Enkidu:

51“I gaze upon thee, O Enkidu, like a god art thou!

52Why with the cattle

53Dost thou [roam] across the field?

54Come, let me lead thee

55into [Erech] of the plazas,

56to the holy house, the dwelling of Anu,

57O, Enkidu arise, let me conduct thee

58To Eanna, the dwelling of Anu,

59The place [where Gish is, perfect] in vitality.

60And thou [like a wife wilt embrace] him.

61Thou [wilt love him like] thyself.

62Come, arise from the ground

63(that is) cursed."

64He heard her word and accepted her speech.

65The counsel of the woman

66Entered his heart.

67She stripped off a garment,

68Clothed him with one.

69Another garment

70She kept on herself.

71She took hold of his hand.

72Like [a god(?)] she brought him

73To the fertile meadow,

74The place of the sheepfolds.

75In that place they received food;

76[For he, Enkidu, whose birthplace was the mountain,]

77[With the gazelles he was accustomed to eat herbs,]

78[With the cattle to drink water,]

79[With the water beings he was happy.]

(Perhaps one additional line missing.)

Col. III.

81Milk of the cattle

82He was accustomed to suck.

83Food they placed before him,

84He broke (it) off and looked

85And gazed.

86Enkidu had not known

87To eat food.

88To drink wine

89He had not been taught.
90The woman opened her mouth and
91Spoke to Enkidu:
92"Eat food, O Enkidu,
93The provender of life!
94Drink wine, the custom of the land!"
95Enkidu ate food
96Till he was satiated.
97Wine he drank,
98Seven goblets.
99His spirit was loosened, he became hilarious.
100His heart became glad and
101His face shone.
102[The barber(?)] removed
103The hair on his body.
104He was anointed with oil.
105He became manlike.
106He put on a garment,
107He was like a man.
108He took his weapon;
109Lions he attacked,
110(so that) the night shepherds could rest.
111He plunged the dagger;
112Lions he overcame.
113The great [shepherds] lay down;
114Enkidu was their protector.
115The strong man,

116The unique hero,

117To [the shepherds(?)] he speaks:

(About five lines missing.)

Col. IV.

(About eight lines missing.)

131Making merry.

132He lifted up his eyes,

133He sees the man.

134He spoke to the woman:

135"O, courtesan, lure on the man.

136Why has he come to me?

137His name I will destroy."

138The woman called to the man

139Who approaches to him[3] and he beholds him.

140"Away! why dost thou [quake(?)]

141Evil is the course of thy activity."[4]

142Then he[5] opened his mouth and

143Spoke to Enkidu:

144"[To have (?)] a family home

145Is the destiny of men, and

146The prerogative(?) of the nobles.

147For the city(?) load the workbaskets!

148Food supply for the city lay to one side!

149For the King of Erech of the plazas,

150Open the hymen(?), perform the marriage act!

151For Gish, the King of Erech of the plazas,

152Open the hymen(?),

153Perform the marriage act!

154With the legitimate wife one should cohabit.

155So before,

156As well as in the future.6

157By the decree pronounced by a god,

158From the cutting of his umbilical cord

159(Such) is his fate."

160At the speech of the hero

161His face grew pale.

(About three lines missing.)

Col. V.

(About six lines missing.)

171[Enkidu] went [in front],

172And the courtesan behind him.

173He entered into Erech of the plazas.

174The people gathered about him.

175As he stood in the streets

176Of Erech of the plazas,

177The men gathered,

178Saying in regard to him:

179"Like the form of Gish he has suddenly become;

180shorter in stature.

181[In his structure high(?)], powerful,

182.......... overseeing(?)

183In the land strong of power has he become.

184Milk of cattle

185He was accustomed to suck."

186Steadily(?) in Erech .....

187The heroes rejoiced.

188He became a leader.

189To the hero of fine appearance,

190To Gish, like a god,

191He became a rival to him.[7]

192For Ishḫara a couch

193Was stretched, and

194Gish [lay down, and afterwards(?)]

195In the night he fled.

196He approaches and

197[Enkidu stood] in the streets.

198He blocked the path

199of Gish.

200At the exhibit of his power,

(About three lines missing.)

Col. VI.

(About four lines missing.)

208Strong(?) …

209Gish

210Against him [Enkidu proceeded],

211[His hair] luxuriant.

212He started [to go]

213Towards him.

214They met in the plaza of the district.

215Enkidu blocked the gate

216With his foot,

217Not permitting Gish to enter.

218They seized (each other), like oxen,

219They fought.

220The threshold they demolished;

221The wall they impaired.

222Gish and Enkidu

223Seized (each other).

224Like oxen they fought.

225The threshold they demolished;

226The wall they impaired.

227Gish bent

228His foot to the ground,[8]

229His wrath was appeased,

230His breast was quieted.

231When his breast was quieted,

232Enkidu to him

233Spoke, to Gish:

234"As a unique one, thy mother

235bore thee.

236The wild cow of the stall,[9]

237Ninsun,

238Has exalted thy head above men.

239Kingship over men

240Enlil has decreed for thee.

241Second tablet,

242enlarged beyond [the original(?)].

243240 lines.

1 I.e., paid homage to the meteor.

2 I.e., the heroes of Erech raised me to my feet, or perhaps in the sense of "supported me."

3 I.e., Enkidu.

4 I.e., "thy way of life."

5 I.e., the man.

6 I.e., an idiomatic phrase meaning "for all times."

7 I.e., Enkidu became like Gish, godlike. Cf. col. 2, 11.

8 He was thrown and therefore vanquished.

9 Epithet given to Ninsun. See the commentary to the line.

Commentary on the Pennsylvania Tablet.

Line 1. The verb *tibû* with *pašâru* expresses the aim of Gish to secure an interpretation for his dream. This disposes of Langdon's note 1 on page 211 of his edition, in which he also erroneously speaks of our text as "late." *Pašâru* is not a variant of *zakâru*. Both verbs occur just as here in the Assyrian version I, 5, 25.

Line 3. *ina šât mušitia*, "in this my night," i.e., in the course of this night of mine. A curious way of putting it, but the expression occurs also in the Assyrian version, e.g., I, 5, 26 (parallel passage to ours) and II, 4[a], 14. In the Yale tablet we find, similarly, *mu-ši-it-ka* (l. 262), "thy night," i.e., "at night to thee."

Line 5. Before Langdon put down the strange statement of Gish "wandering about in the midst of omens" (misreading *id-da-tim* for *it-lu-tim*), he might have asked himself the question, what it could possibly mean. How can one walk among omens?

Line 6. *ka-ka-bu šá-ma-i* must be taken as a compound term for "starry heaven." The parallel passage in the Assyrian version (Tablet I, 5, 27) has the ideograph for star, with the plural sign as a variant. Literally, therefore, "The starry heaven (or "the stars in heaven") was there," etc. Langdon's note 2 on page 211 rests on an erroneous reading.

Line 7. *kiṣru šá Anim*, "mass of Anu," appears to be the designation of a meteor, which might well be described as a "mass" coming from Anu, i.e., from the god of heaven who becomes the personification of the heavens in general. In the Assyrian version (I, 5, 28) we have *kima ki-iṣ-rù*, i.e., "something like a mass of heaven." Note also I, 3, 16, where in a description of Gilgamesh, his strength is said to be "strong like a mass (i.e., a meteor) of heaven."

Line 9. For *nuššašu ûl iltê* we have a parallel in the Hebrew phrase נִלְפָּסֵתִי נִשַּׂפָּס (Isaiah 1, 14).

Line 10. *Uruk mâtum*, as the designation for the district of Erech, occurs in the Assyrian version, e.g., I, 5, 31, and IV, 2, 38; also to be supplied, I, 6, 23.

For *paḫir* the parallel in the Assyrian version has *iz-za-az* (I, 5, 31), but VI, 197, we find *paḫ-ru* and *paḫ-ra*.

Line 17. *mi-in-di* does not mean "truly" as Langdon translates, but "some one." It occurs also in the Assyrian version X, 1, 13, *mi-in-di-e ma-an-nu-ṵ*, "this is some one who," etc.

Line 18. Cf. Assyrian version I, 5, 3, and IV, 4, 7, *ina ṣiri âlid*—both passages referring to Enkidu.

Line 21. Cf. Assyrian version II, 3^b, 38, with *malkê*, "kings," as a synonym of *itlutum*.

Line 23. *ta-tar-ra-as-sú* from *tarâṣu*, "direct," "guide," etc.

Line 24. I take *uš-ti-nim-ma* as III, 2, from *išênu* (יָשֵׁן), the verb underlying *šittu*, "sleep," and *šuttu*, "dream."

Line 26. Cf. Assyrian version I, 6, 21—a complete parallel.

Line 28. *Uruk ri-bi-tim*, the standing phrase in both tablets of the old Babylonian version, for which in the Assyrian version we have *Uruk su-pu-ri*. The former term suggests the "broad space" outside of the city or the "common" in a village community, while *supûri*, "enclosed," would refer to the city within the walls. Dr. W. F. Albright (in a private communication) suggests "Erech of the plazas" as a suitable translation for *Uruk ribîtim*. A third term, *Uruk mâtum* (see above, note to line 10), though designating rather the district of which Erech was the capital, appears to be used as a synonym to *Uruk ribîtim*, as may be concluded from the phrase *i-na ri-bi-tum ma-ti* (l. 214 of the Pennsylvania tablet), which clearly means the "plaza" of the city. One naturally thinks of רְחֹבֹת עִיר in Genesis 10, 11—the equivalent of Babylonian *ri-bi-tu âli*—which can hardly be the name of a city. It appears to be a gloss, as is הִיא הָעִיר הַגְּדֹלָה at the end of v. 12. The latter gloss is misplaced, since it clearly describes "Nineveh," mentioned in v. 11. Inasmuch as רְחֹבֹת עִיר immediately follows the mention of Nineveh, it seems simplest to take the phrase as designating the "outside" or "suburbs" of the city, a complete parallel, therefore, to *ri-bi-tu mâti* in our text. Nineveh, together with the "suburbs," forms the "great city." *Uruk ribîtim* is, therefore, a designation for "greater Erech," proper to a capital city, which by its gradual growth would take in more than its original confines. "Erech of the plazas" must have come to be used as a honorific designation of this important center as early as 2000 B. C., whereas later, perhaps because of its decline, the epithet no longer seemed appropriate and was replaced by the more modest designation of "walled Erech," with an allusion to the tradition which ascribed the building of the wall of the city to Gilgamesh. At all events, all three expressions, "Erech of the plazas," "Erech walled" and "Erech land," are to be regarded as synonymous. The position once held by Erech follows also from its ideographic designation (Brünnow No. 4796) by the sign "house" with a "gunufied" extension, which conveys the idea of Unu = *šubtu*, or "dwelling" *par excellence*. The pronunciation Unug or Unuk (see the gloss *u-nu-uk*, VR 23, 8[a]), composed of *unu*, "dwelling," and *ki*, "place," is hardly to be regarded as older than Uruk, which is to be resolved into *uru*, "city," and *ki*, "place," but rather as a play upon the name, both Unu + ki and Uru + ki conveying the same idea of *the* city or *the* dwelling place *par excellence*. As the seat of the second oldest dynasty according to Babylonian traditions (see Poebel's list in *Historical and Grammatical Texts* No. 2), Erech no doubt was regarded as having been at one time "the city," i.e., the capital of the entire Euphrates Valley.

Line 31. A difficult line for which Langdon proposes the translation: "Another axe seemed his visage"!!—which may be picturesque, but hardly a description befitting a hero. How can a man's face seem to be an axe? Langdon attaches *šá-ni* in the sense of "second" to the preceding word "axe," whereas *šanî bunušu*, "change of his countenance" or "his countenance being changed," is to be taken as a phrase to convey the idea of "being disturbed," "displeased" or "angry." The phrase is of the same kind as the well-known *šunnu ṭêmu*, "changing of reason," to denote "insanity." See the passages in Muss-Arnolt, *Assyrian Dictionary*, pp. 355 and 1068. In Hebrew, too, we have the same two phrases, e.g., וַיְשַׁנּוֹ אֶת־טַעְמוֹ (I Sam. 21, 14 = Ps. 34, 1), "and he changed his reason," i.e., feigned insanity and מְשַׁנֶּה פָנָיו (Job 14, 20), "changing his face," to indicate a radical alteration in the frame of mind. There is a still closer parallel in Biblical Aramaic: Dan. 3, 19, "The form of his visage was changed," meaning "he was enraged." Fortunately, the same phrase occurs also in the Yale tablet (l. 192), *šá-nu-ú bu-nu-šú*, in a connection which leaves no doubt that the aroused fury of the tyrant Ḫuwawa is described by it:

"Ḫuwawa heard and his face was changed"

precisely, therefore, as we should say—following Biblical usage—"his countenance fell." Cf. also the phrase *pânušu arpu*, "his countenance was darkened" (Assyrian version I, 2, 48), to express "anger." The line, therefore, in the Pennsylvania tablet must describe Enkidu's anger. With the brandishing of the axe the hero's anger was also stirred up. The touch was added to prepare us for the continuation in which Gish describes how, despite this (or perhaps just because of it), Enkidu seemed so attractive that Gish instantly fell in love with him. May perhaps the emphatic form *ḫaṢinumma* (line 31) against *ḫaṢinu* (line 29) have been used to indicate "The axe it was," or "because of the axe?" It would be worth while to examine other texts of the Hammurabi period with a view of determining the scope in the use and meaning of the emphatic *ma* when added to a substantive.

Line 32. The combination *amur ù aḫtadu* occurs also in the El-Amarna Letters, No. 18, 12.

Line 34. In view of the common Hebrew, Syriac and Arabic חָבַב "to love," it seems preferable to read here, as in the other passages in the Assyrian versions (I, 4, 15; 4, 35; 6, 27, etc.), *a-ḫa-ab-bu-ub*, *aḫ-bu-ub*, *iḫ-bu-bu*, etc. (instead of with *p*), and to render "embrace."

Lines 38–40, completing the column, may be supplied from the Assyrian version I, 6, 30–32, in conjunction with lines 33–34 of our text. The beginning of line 32 in Jensen's version is therefore to be filled out *[ta-ra-am-šú ki]-i.*

Line 43. The restoration at the beginning of this line

En-ki-[dũ wa]-ši-ib ma-ḫar ḫa-ri-im-tim

enables us to restore also the beginning of the second tablet of the Assyrian version (cf. the colophon of the fragment 81, 7–27, 93, in Jeremias, *Izdubar-Nimrod*, plate IV = Jensen, p. 134),

[^{d}En-ki-dũ wa-ši-ib] ma-ḫar-šá.

Line 44. The restoration of this line is largely conjectural, based on the supposition that its contents correspond in a general way to I, 4, 16, of the Assyrian version. The reading *di-da* is quite certain, as is also *ip-ti-[e]*; and since both words occur in the line of the Assyrian version in question, it is tempting to supply at the beginning *ur-[šá]* = "her loins" (cf. Holma, *Namen der Körperteile*, etc., p. 101), which is likewise found in the same line of the Assyrian version. At all events the line describes the fascination exercised upon Enkidu by the woman's bodily charms, which make him forget everything else.

Lines 46–47 form a parallel to I, 4, 21, of the Assyrian version. The form *šamkatu*, "courtesan," is constant in the old Babylonian version (ll. 135 and 172), as against *šamḫatu* in the Assyrian version (I, 3, 19, 40, 45; 4, 16), which also uses the plural *šam-ḫa-a-ti* (II, 3^{b}, 40). The interchange between *ḫ* and *k* is not without precedent (cf. Meissner, *Altbabylonisches Privatrecht*, page 107, note 2, and more particularly Chiera, *List of Personal Names*, page 37).

In view of the evidence, set forth in the Introduction, for the assumption that the Enkidu story has been combined with a tale of the evolution of primitive man to civilized life, it is reasonable to suggest that in the original Enkidu story the female companion was called *šamkatu*, "courtesan," whereas in the tale of the primitive man, which was transferred to Enkidu, the associate was *ḫarimtu*, a "woman," just as in the Genesis tale, the companion of Adam is simply called *ishshâ*, "woman." Note that in the Assyrian parallel (Tablet I, 4, 26) we have two readings, *ir-ḫi* (imperf.) and a variant *i-ri-ḫi* (present). The former is the better reading, as our tablet shows.

Lines 49–59 run parallel to the Assyrian version I, 4, 33–38, with slight variations which have been discussed above, p. 58, and from which we may conclude that the Assyrian version represents an independent redaction. Since in our tablet we have presumably the repetition of what may have been in part at least set forth in the first tablet of the old Babylonian version, we must not press the parallelism with the first tablet of the Assyrian version too far; but it is noticeable nevertheless (1) that our tablet contains lines 57–58 which are not represented in the Assyrian version, and (2) that the second speech of the "woman" beginning, line 62, with *al-ka*, "come" (just as the first speech, line 54), is likewise not found in the first tablet of the Assyrian version; which on the other hand contains a line (39) not in the Babylonian version, besides the detailed answer of Enkidu (I 4, 42–5, 5). Line 6, which reads "Enkidu and the woman went (*il-li-ku*) to walled Erech," is also not found in the second tablet of the old Babylonian version.

Line 63. For *magrû*, "accursed," see the frequent use in Astrological texts (Jastrow, *Religion Babyloniens und Assyriens* II, page 450, note 2). Langdon, by his strange error in separating *ma-a-ag-ri-im* into two words *ma-a-ak* and *ri-i-im*, with a still stranger rendering: "unto the place yonder of the shepherds!!", naturally misses the point of this important speech.

Line 64 corresponds to I, 4, 40, of the Assyrian version, which has an additional line, leading to the answer of Enkidu. From here on, our tablet furnishes material not represented in the Assyrian version, but which was no doubt included in the second tablet of that version of which we have only a few fragments.

Line 70 must be interpreted as indicating that the woman kept one garment for herself. *Ittalbaš* would accordingly mean, "she kept on." The female dress appears to have consisted of an upper and a lower garment.

Line 72. The restoration "like a god" is favored by line 51, where Enkidu is likened to a god, and is further confirmed by l. 190.

Line 73. *gupru* is identical with *gu-up-ri* (Thompson, *Reports of the Magicians and Astrologers*, etc., 223 rev. 2 and 223[a] rev. 8), and must be correlated to *gipâru* (Muss-Arnolt, *Assyrian Dictionary*, p. 229[a]), "planted field," "meadow," and the like. Thompson's translation "men" (as though a synonym of *gabru*) is to be corrected accordingly.

Line 74. There is nothing missing between *a-šar* and *tar-ba-ṣi-im*.

Line 75. *ri-ia-ú*, which Langdon renders "shepherd," is the equivalent of the Arabic *riʿy* and Hebrew רְעִי "pasturage," "fodder." We have usually the feminine form *ri-i-tu* (Muss-Arnolt, *Assyrian Dictionary*, p. 990[b]). The break at the end of the second column is not serious. Evidently Enkidu, still accustomed to live like an animal, is first led to the sheepfolds, and this suggests a repetition of the description of his former life. Of the four or five lines missing, we may conjecturally restore four, on the basis of the Assyrian version, Tablet I, 4, 2–5, or I, 2, 39–41. This would then join on well to the beginning of column 3.

Line 81. Both here and in l. 52 our text has *na-ma-áš-te-e*, as against *nam-maš-ši-i* in the Assyrian version, e.g., Tablet I, 2, 41; 4, 5, etc.,—the feminine form, therefore, as against the masculine. Langdon's note 3 on page 213 is misleading. In astrological texts we also find *nam-maš-te*; e.g., Thompson, *Reports of the Magicians and Astrologers*, etc., No. 200, Obv. 2.

Line 93. *ẓi-ma-at* (for *simat*) *ba-la-ṭi-im* is not "conformity of life" as Langdon renders, but that which "belongs to life" like *si-mat pag-ri-šá*, "belonging to her body," in the Assyrian version III, 2[a], 3 (Jensen, page 146). "Food," says the woman, "is the staff of life."

Line 94. Langdon's strange rendering "of the conditions and fate of the land" rests upon an erroneous reading (see the corrections, Appendix I), which is the more inexcusable because in line 97 the same ideogram, Kàš = *šikaru*, "wine," occurs, and is correctly rendered by him. *Šimti mâti* is not the "fate of the land," but the "fixed custom of the land."

Line 98. *aṢ-Ṣa-mi-im* (plural of *aṢṢamu*), which Langdon takes as an adverb in the sense of "times," is a well-known word for a large "goblet," which occurs in Incantation texts, e.g., *CT* XVI, 24, obv. 1, 19, *mê a-Ṣa-am-mi-e šú-puk*, "pour out goblets of water." Line 18 of the passage shoves that *aṢammu* is a Sumerian loan word.

Line 99. *it-tap-šar*, I, 2, from *pašâru*, "loosen." In combination with *kabtatum* (from *kabitatum*, yielding two forms: *kabtatum*, by elision of *i*, and *kabittu*, by elision of *a*), "liver," *pašâru* has the force of becoming cheerful. Cf. *ka-bit-ta-ki lip-pa-šir* (*ZA* V., p. 67, line 14).

Line 100, note the customary combination of "liver" (*kabtatum*) and "heart" (*libbu*) for "disposition" and "mind," just as in the standing phrase in penitential prayers: "May thy liver be appeased, thy heart be quieted."

Line 102. The restoration [[lù]ŠÚ]-I = *gallabu* "barber" (Delitzsch, *Sumer. Glossar*, p. 267) was suggested to me by Dr. H. F. Lutz. The ideographic writing "raising the hand" is interesting as recalling the gesture of shaving or cutting. Cf. a reference to a barber in Lutz, *Early Babylonian Letters from Larsa*, No. 109, 6.

Line 103. Langdon has correctly rendered *šuḫuru* as "hair," and has seen that we have here a loan-word from the Sumerian Suḫur = *kimmatu*, "hair," according to the Syllabary S^b 357 (cf. Delitzsch, *Sumer. Glossar.*, p. 253). For *kimmatu*, "hair," more specifically hair of the head and face, see Holma, *Namen der Körperteile*, page 3. The same sign Suḫur or Suḫ (Brünnow No. 8615), with Lal, i.e., "hanging hair," designates the "beard" (*ziḳnu*, cf. Brünnow, No. 8620, and Holma, l. c., p. 36), and it is interesting to note that we have *šuḫuru* (introduced as a loan-word) for the barbershop, according to II R, 21, 27^c (= *CT* XII, 41).

Ê suḫur(ra) (i.e., house of the hair) = *šú-ḫu-ru.*

In view of all this, we may regard as assured Holma's conjecture to read *šú-[ḫur-ma-šú]* in the list 93074 obv. (*MVAG* 1904, p. 203; and Holma, *Beiträge z. Assyr. Lexikon*, p. 36), as the Akkadian equivalent to Suḫur-Maš-Ḫa and the name of a fish, so called because it appeared to have a double "beard" (cf. Holma, *Namen der Körperteile*). One is tempted, furthermore, to see in the difficult word שכירה (Isaiah 7, 20) a loan-word from our *šuḫuru*, and to take the words פֶּסֶת־הָרַפָּסֹשׁ וְשַׂעַר הָרַגְלָיִם "the head and hair of the feet" (euphemistic for the hair around the privates), as an explanatory gloss to the rare word שכירה for "hair" of the body in general—just as in the passage in the Pennsylvania tablet. The verse in Isaiah would then read, "The Lord on that day will shave with the razor the hair (השכירה), and even the beard will be removed." The rest of the verse would represent a series of explanatory glosses: (a) "Beyond the river" (i.e., Assyria), a gloss to יְגַלַּח (b) "with the king of Assyria," a gloss to בְּתַעַר "with a razor;" and (c) "the hair of the head and hair of the feet," a gloss to השכירה. For "hair of the feet" we have an interesting equivalent in Babylonian *šu-ḫur* (and *šú-ḫu-ur*) *šêpi* (*CT* XII, 41, 23–24 c-d). Cf. also Boissier, *Documents Assyriens relatifs aux Présages*, p. 258, 4–5. The Babylonian phrase is like the Hebrew one to be interpreted as a euphemism for the hair around the male or female organ. To be sure, the change from ה to כ in השכירה constitutes an objection, but not a serious one in the case of a loan-word, which would aim to give the *pronunciation* of the original word, rather than the correct etymological equivalent. The writing with aspirated כ fulfills this condition. (Cf. *šamkatum* and *šamḫatum*, above p. 73). The passage in Isaiah being a reference to Assyria, the prophet might be tempted to use a foreign word to make his point more emphatic. To take השכירה as "hired," as has hitherto been done, and to translate "with a hired razor," is not only to suppose a very wooden metaphor, but is grammatically difficult, since השכירה would be a feminine adjective attached to a masculine substantive.

Coming back to our passage in the Pennsylvania tablet, it is to be noted that Enkidu is described as covered "all over his body with hair" (Assyrian version, Tablet I, 2, 36) like an animal. To convert him into a civilized man, the hair is removed.

Line 107. *mutu* does not mean "husband" here, as Langdon supposes, but must be taken as in l. 238 in the more general sense of "man," for which there is good evidence.

Line 109. *la-bi* (plural form) are "lions"—not "panthers" as Langdon has it. The verb *ú-gi-ir-ri* is from *gâru*, "to attack." Langdon by separating *ú* from *gi-ir-ri* gets a totally wrong and indeed absurd meaning. See the corrections in the Appendix. He takes the sign *ú* for the copula (!!) which of course is impossible.

Line 110. Read *uš-sa-ak-pu*, III, 1, of *sakâpu*, which is frequently used for "lying down" and is in fact a synonym of *ṣalâlu*. See Muss-Arnolt, *Assyrian Dictionary*, page 758[a]. The original has very clearly Síb (= *rê'u*, "shepherd") with the plural sign. The "shepherds of the night," who could now rest since Enkidu had killed the lions, are of course the shepherds who were accustomed to watch the flocks during the night.

Line 111. *ut-tap-pi-iš* is II, 2, *napâšu*, "to make a hole," hence "to plunge" in connection with a weapon. *Šib-ba-ri* is, of course, not "mountain goats," as Langdon renders, but a by-form to *šibbiru*, "stick," and designates some special weapon. Since on seal cylinders depicting Enkidu killing lions and other animals the hero is armed with a dagger, this is presumably the weapon *šibbaru*.

Line 113. Langdon's translation is again out of the question and purely fanciful. The traces favor the restoration *na-ki-[di-e]*, "shepherds," and since the line appears to be a parallel to line 110, I venture to suggest at the beginning *[it-ti]-lu* from *na'âlu*, "lie down"—a synonym, therefore, to *sakâpu* in line 110. The shepherds can sleep quietly after Enkidu has become the "guardian" of the flocks. In the Assyrian version (tablet II, 3[a], 4) Enkidu is called a *na-kid*, "shepherd," and in the preceding line we likewise have [lù]Na-Kid with the plural sign, i.e., "shepherds." This would point to *nakidu* being a Sumerian loan-word, unless it is *vice versa*, a word that has gone over into the Sumerian from Akkadian. Is perhaps the fragment in question (K 8574) in the Assyrian version (Haupt's ed. No. 25) the *parallel* to our passage? If in line 4 of this fragment we could read *šú* for *sa*, i.e., *na-kid-šú-nu*, "their shepherd, we would have a parallel to line 114 of the Pennsylvania tablet, with *na-kid* as a synonym to *maṢṢaru*, "protector." The preceding line would then be completed as follows:

[it-ti-lu]-nim-ma na-kid[meš] [ra-bu-tum]

(or perhaps only *it-ti-lu-ma*, since the *nim* is not certain) and would correspond to line 113 of the Pennsylvania tablet. Inasmuch as the writing on the tiny fragment is very much blurred, it is quite possible that in line 2 we must read *šib-ba-ri* (instead of *bar-ba-ri*), which would furnish a parallel to line 111 of the Pennsylvania tablet. The difference between Bar and Šib is slight, and the one sign might easily be mistaken for the other in the case of close writing. The continuation of line 2 of the fragment would then correspond to line 112 of the Pennsylvania tablet, while line 1 of the fragment might be completed *[re-e]-u-ti(?) šá [mu-ši-a-tim]*, though this is by no means certain.

The break at the close of column 3 (about 5 lines) and the top of column 4 (about 8 lines) is a most serious interruption in the narrative, and makes it difficult to pick up the thread where the tablet again becomes readable. We cannot be certain whether the "strong man, the unique hero" who addresses some one (lines 115–117) is Enkidu or Gish or some other personage, but presumably Gish is meant. In the Assyrian version, Tablet I, 3, 2 and 29, we find Gilgamesh described as the "unique hero" and in l. 234 of the Pennsylvania tablet Gish is called "unique," while again, in the Assyrian version, Tablet I, 2, 15 and 26, he is designated as *gašru* as in our text. Assuming this, whom does he address? Perhaps the shepherds? In either case he receives an answer that rejoices him. If the fragment of the Assyrian version (K 8574) above discussed is the equivalent to the close of column 3 of the Pennsylvania tablet, we may go one step further, and with some measure of assurance assume that Gish is told of Enkidu's exploits and that the latter is approaching Erech. This pleases Gish, but Enkidu when he sees Gish(?) is stirred to anger and wants to annihilate him. At this point, the "man" (who is probably Gish, though the possibility of a third personage must be admitted) intervenes and in a long speech sets forth the destiny and higher aims of mankind. The contrast between Enkidu and Gish (or the third party) is that between the primitive savage and the civilized being. The contrast is put in the form of an opposition between the two. The primitive man is the stronger and wishes to destroy the one whom he regards as a natural foe and rival. On the other hand, the one who stands on a higher plane wants to lift his fellow up. The whole of column 4, therefore, forms part of the lesson attached to the story of Enkidu, who, identified with man in a primitive stage, is made the medium of illustrating how the higher plane is reached through the guiding influences of the woman's hold on man, an influence exercised, to be sure, with the help of her bodily charms.

Line 135. *uk-ki-ši* (imperative form) does not mean "take away," as Langdon (who entirely misses the point of the whole passage) renders, but on the contrary, "lure him on," "entrap him," and the like. The verb occurs also in the Yale tablet, ll. 183 and 186.

Line 137. Langdon's note to *lu-uš-šú* had better be passed over in silence. The form is II. 1, from *ešû*, "destroy."

Line 139. Since the man whom the woman calls approaches Enkidu, the subject of both verbs is the man, and the object is Enkidu; i.e., therefore, "The man approaches Enkidu and beholds him."

Line 140. Langdon's interpretation of this line again is purely fanciful. *E-di-il* cannot, of course, be a "phonetic variant" of *edir*; and certainly the line does not describe the state of mind of the woman. Lines 140–141 are to be taken as an expression of amazement at Enkidu's appearance. The first word appears to be an imperative in the sense of "Be off," "Away," from *dâlu*, "move, roam." The second word *e-eš*, "why," occurs with the same verb *dâlu* in the Meissner fragment: *e-eš ta-da-al* (column 3, 1), "why dost thou roam about?" The verb at the end of the line may perhaps be completed to *ta-ḫi-il-la-am*. The last sign appears to be *am*, but may be *ma*, in which case we should have to complete simply *ta-ḫi-il-ma*. *Taḫîl* would be the second person present of *ḫîlu*. Cf. *i-ḫi-il*, frequently in astrological texts, e.g., Virolleaud, *Adad* No. 3, lines 21 and 33.

Line 141. The reading *lim-nu* at the beginning, instead of Langdon's *mi-nu*, is quite certain, as is also *ma-na-aḫ-ti-ka* instead of what Langdon proposes, which gives no sense whatever. *Manaḫtu* in the sense of the "toil" and "activity of life" (like עָמָל throughout the Book of Ecclesiastes) occurs in the introductory lines to the Assyrian version of the Epic I, 1, 8, *ka-lu ma-na-aḫ-ti-[šu]*, "all of his toil," i.e., all of his career.

Line 142. The subject of the verb cannot be the woman, as Langdon supposes, for the text in that case, e.g., line 49, would have said *pi-šá* ("her mouth") not *pi-šú* ("his mouth"). The long speech, detailing the function and destiny of civilized man, is placed in the mouth of the man who meets Enkidu.

In the Introduction it has been pointed out that lines 149 and 151 of the speech appear to be due to later modifications of the speech designed to connect the episode with Gish. Assuming this to be the case, the speech sets forth the following five distinct aims of human life: (1) establishing a home (line 144), (2) work (line 147), (3) storing up resources (line 148), (4) marriage (line 150), (5) monogamy (line 154); all of which is put down as established for all time by divine decree (lines 155–157), and as man's fate from his birth (lines 158–159).

Line 144. *bi-ti-iš e-mu-ti* is for *bîti šá e-mu-ti*, just as *ḳab-lu-uš Ti-a-ma-ti* (Assyrian Creation Myth, IV, 65) stands for *ḳablu šá Tiamti*. Cf. *bît e-mu-ti* (Assyrian version, IV, 2, 46 and 48). The end of the line is lost beyond recovery, but the general sense is clear.

Line 146. *tu-a-ar* is a possible reading. It may be the construct of *tu-a-ru*, of frequent occurrence in legal texts and having some such meaning as "right," "claim" or "prerogative." See the passages given by Muss-Arnolt, *Assyrian Dictionary*, p. 1139^{b}.

Line 148. The reading *uk-la-at*, "food," and then in the wider sense "food supply," "provisions," is quite certain. The fourth sign looks like the one for "city." *E-mi-sa* may stand for *e-mid-sa*, "place it." The general sense of the line, at all events, is clear, as giving the advice to gather resources. It fits in with the Babylonian outlook on life to regard work and wealth as the fruits of work and as a proper purpose in life.

Line 150 (repeated lines 152–153) is a puzzling line. To render *piti pûk epši* (or *epiši*), as Langdon proposes, "open, addressing thy speech," is philologically and in every other respect inadmissible. The word *pu-uk* (which Langdon takes for "thy mouth"!!) can, of course, be nothing but the construct form of *pukku*, which occurs in the Assyrian version in the sense of "net" (*pu-uk-ku* I, 2, 9 and 21, and also in the colophon to the eleventh tablet furnishing the beginning of the twelfth tablet (Haupt's edition No. 56), as well as in column 2, 29, and column 3, 6, of this twelfth tablet). In the two last named passages *pukku* is a synonym of *mekû*, which from the general meaning of "enclosure" comes to be a euphemistic expression for the female organ. So, for example, in the Assyrian Creation Myth, Tablet IV, 66 (synonym of *ḳablu*, "waist," etc.). See Holma, *Namen der Körperteile*, page 158. Our word *pukku* must be taken in this same sense as a designation of the female organ—perhaps more specifically the "hymen" as the "net," though the womb in general might also be designated as a "net" or "enclosure." *Kak-(ši)* is no doubt to be read *epši*, as Langdon correctly saw; or perhaps better, *epiši*. An expression like *ip-ši-šú lul-la-a* (Assyrian version, I, 4, 13; also line 19, *i-pu-us-su-ma lul-la-a*), with the explanation *šipir zinništi*, "the work of woman" (i.e., after the fashion of woman), shows that *epêšu* is used in connection with the sexual act. The phrase *pitî pûk epiši a-na ḫa-a-a-ri*, literally "open the net, perform the act for marriage," therefore designates the fulfillment of the marriage act, and the line is intended to point to marriage with the accompanying sexual intercourse as one of the duties of man. While the general meaning is thus clear, the introduction of Gish is puzzling, except on the supposition that lines 149 and 151 represent later additions to connect the speech, detailing the advance to civilized life, with the hero. See above, p. 45 *seq.*

Line 154. *aššat šimâtim* is the "legitimate wife," and the line inculcates monogamy as against promiscuous sexual intercourse. We know that monogamy was the rule in Babylonia, though a man could in addition to the wife recognized as the legalized spouse take a concubine, or his wife could give her husband a slave as a concubine. Even in that case, according to the Hammurabi Code, §§145–146, the wife retained her status. The Code throughout assumes that a man has only *one* wife—

the *aššat šimâtim* of our text. The phrase "so" (or "that") before "as afterwards" is to be taken as an idiomatic expression—"so it was and so it should be for all times"—somewhat like the phrase *maḫriam ù arkiam*, "for all times," in legal documents (*CT* VIII, 38^{c}, 22–23). For the use of *mûk* see Behrens, *Assyrisch-Babylonische Briefe*, p. 3.

Line 158. *i-na bi-ti-iḳ a-bu-un-na-ti-šú.* Another puzzling line, for which Langdon proposes "in the work of his presence," which is as obscure as the original. In a note he says that *apunnâti* means "nostrils," which is certainly wrong. There has been considerable discussion about this term (see Holma, *Namen der Körperteile*, pages 150 and 157), the meaning of which has been advanced by Christian's discussion in *OLZ* 1914, p. 397. From this it appears that it must designate a part of the body which could acquire a wider significance so as to be used as a synonym for "totality," since it appears in a list of equivalent for Dur = *nap-ḫa-ru*, "totality," *ka-lu-ma*, "all," *a-bu-un-na-tum e-ṣi-im-tum*, "bony structure," and *kul-la-tum*, "totality" (*CT* XII, 10, 7–10). Christian shows that it may be the "navel," which could well acquire a wider significance for the body in general; but we may go a step further and specify the "umbilical cord" (tentatively suggested also by Christian) as the primary meaning, then the "navel," and from this the "body" in general. The structure of the umbilical cord as a series of strands would account for designating it by a plural form *abunnâti*, as also for the fact that one could speak of a right and left side of the *appunnâti*. To distinguish between the "umbilical cord" and the "navel," the ideograph Dur (the common meaning of which is *riksu*, "bond" [Delitzsch, *Sumer. Glossar.*, p. 150]), was used for the former, while for the latter Li Dur was employed, though the reading in Akkadian in both cases was the same. The expression "with (or at) the cutting of his umbilical cord" would mean, therefore, "from his birth"—since the cutting of the cord which united the child with the mother marks the beginning of the separate life. Lines 158–159, therefore, in concluding the address to Enkidu, emphasize in a picturesque way that what has been set forth is man's fate for which he has been destined from birth. [See now Albright's remarks on *abunnatu* in the Revue d'Assyriologie 16, pp. 173–175, with whose conclusion, however, that it means primarily "backbone" and then "stature," I cannot agree.]

In the break of about three lines at the bottom of column 4, and of about six at the beginning of column 5, there must have been set forth the effect of the address on Enkidu and the indication of his readiness to accept the advice; as in a former passage (line 64), Enkidu showed himself willing to follow the woman. At all events the two now proceed to the heart of the city. Enkidu is in front and the woman behind him. The scene up to this point must have taken place outside of Erech—in the suburbs or approaches to the city, where the meadows and the sheepfolds were situated.

Line 174. *um-ma-nu-um* are not the "artisans," as Langdon supposes, but the "people" of Erech, just as in the Assyrian version, Tablet IV, 1, 40, where the word occurs in connection with *i-dip-pi-ir*, which is perhaps to be taken as a synonym of *paḫâru*, "gather;" so also *i-dip-pir* (Tablet I, 2, 40) "gathers with the flock."

Lines 180–182 must have contained the description of Enkidu's resemblance to Gish, but the lines are too mutilated to permit of any certain restoration. See the corrections (Appendix) for a suggested reading for the end of line 181.

Line 183 can be restored with considerable probability on the basis of the Assyrian version, Tablet I, 3, 3 and 30, where Enkidu is described as one "whose power is strong in the land."

Lines 186–187. The puzzling word, to be read apparently *kak-ki-a-tum*, can hardly mean "weapons," as Langdon proposes. In that case we should expect *kakkê*; and, moreover, to so render gives no sense, especially since the verb *ú-te-el-li-lu* is without much question to be rendered "rejoiced," and not "purified." *Kakkiatum*—if this be the correct reading—may be a designation of Erech like *ribîtim*.

Lines 188–189 are again entirely misunderstood by Langdon, owing to erroneous readings. See the corrections in the Appendix.

Line 190. *i-li-im* in this line is used like Hebrew Elohîm, "God."

Line 191. *šakiššum* = *šakin-šum*, as correctly explained by Langdon.

Line 192. With this line a new episode begins which, owing to the gap at the beginning of column 6, is somewhat obscure. The episode leads to the hostile encounter between Gish and Enkidu. It is referred to in column 2 of the fourth tablet of the Assyrian version. Lines 35–50—all that is preserved of this column—form in part a parallel to columns 5–6 of the Pennsylvania tablet, but in much briefer form, since what on the Pennsylvania tablet is the incident itself is on the fourth tablet of the Assyrian version merely a repeated summary of the relationship between the two heroes, leading up to the expedition against Ḫu(m)baba. Lines 38–40 of column 2 of the Assyrian version correspond to lines 174–177 of the Pennsylvania tablet, and lines 44–50 to lines 192–221. It would seem that Gish proceeds stealthily at night to go to the goddess Ishḫara, who lies on a couch in the *bît êmuti* , the "family house" Assyrian version, Tablet IV, 2. 46–48). He encounters Enkidu in the street, and the latter blocks Gish's path, puts his foot in the gate leading to the house where the goddess is, and thus prevents Gish from entering. Thereupon the two have a fierce encounter in which Gish is worsted. The meaning of the episode itself is not clear. Does Enkidu propose to deprive Gish, here viewed as a god (cf. line 190 of the Pennsylvania tablet = Assyrian version, Tablet I, 4, 45, "like a god"), of his spouse, the goddess Ishḫara—another form of Ishtar? Or are the two heroes, the one a counterpart of the other, contesting for the possession of a goddess? Is it in this scene that Enkidu becomes the "rival" (*me-iḫ-rù*, line 191 of the Pennsylvania tablet) of the divine Gish? We must content ourself with having obtained through the Pennsylvania tablet a clearer indication of the occasion of the fight between the two heroes, and leave the further explanation of the episode till a fortunate chance may throw additional light upon it. There is perhaps a reference to the episode in the Assyrian version, Tablet II, 3^{b}, 35–36.

Line 196. For *i-na-ag-šá-am* (from *nagâšu*), Langdon proposes the purely fanciful "embracing her in sleep," whereas it clearly means "he approaches." Cf. Muss-Arnolt, *Assyrian Dictionary*, page 645^{a}.

Lines 197–200 appear to correspond to Tablet IV, 2, 35–37, of the Assyrian version, though not forming a complete parallel. We may therefore supply at the beginning of line 35 of the Assyrian version *[ittaziz] Enkidu*, corresponding to line 197 of the Pennsylvania tablet. Line 36 of IV, 2, certainly appears to correspond to line 200 (*dan-nu-ti = da-na-ni-iš-šú*).

Line 208. The first sign looks more like *šar*, though *ur* is possible.

Line 211 is clearly a description of Enkidu, as is shown by a comparison with the Assyrian version I, 2, 37: *[pi]-ti-ik pi-ir-ti-šú uḫ-tan-na-ba kima* ^{d}*Nidaba*, "The form of his hair sprouted like wheat." We must therefore supply Enkidu in the preceding line. Tablet IV, 4, 6, of the Assyrian version also contains a reference to the flowing hair of Enkidu.

Line 212. For the completion of the line cf. Harper, *Assyrian and Babylonian Letters*, No. 214.

Line 214. For *ribîtu mâti* see the note above to line 28 of column 1.

Lines 215–217 correspond almost entirely to the Assyrian version IV, 2, 46–48. The variations *ki-ib-su* in place of *šêpu*, and *kima lîm*, "like oxen," instead of *ina bâb êmuti* (repeated from line 46), *ana šurûbi* for *êribam*, are slight though interesting. The Assyrian version shows that the "gate" in line 215 is "the gate of the family house" in which the goddess Ishḫara lies.

Lines 218–228. The detailed description of the fight between the two heroes is only partially preserved in the Assyrian version.

Line 218. *li-i-im* is evidently to be taken as plural here as in line 224, just as *su-ḳi-im* (lines 27 and 175), *ri-bi-tim* (lines 4, 28, etc.), *tarbaṢim* (line 74), *aṢṢamim* (line 98) are plural forms. Our text furnishes, as does also the Yale tablet, an interesting illustration of the vacillation in the Hammurabi period in the twofold use of *im*: (a) as an indication of the plural (as in Hebrew), and (b) as a mere emphatic ending (lines 63, 73, and 232), which becomes predominant in the post-Hammurabi age.

Line 227. Gilgamesh is often represented on seal cylinders as kneeling, e.g., Ward Seal Cylinders Nos. 159, 160, 165. Cf. also Assyrian version V, 3, 6, where Gilgamesh is described as kneeling, though here in prayer. See further the commentary to the Yale tablet, line 215.

Line 229. We must of course read *uz-za-šú*, "his anger," and not *uṢ-Ṣa-šú*, "his javelin," as Langdon does, which gives no sense.

Line 231. Langdon's note is erroneous. He again misses the point. The stem of the verb here as in line 230 (*i-ni-iḫ*) is the common *nâḫu*, used so constantly in connection with *pašâḫu*, to designate the cessation of anger.

Line 234. *ištên* applied to Gish designates him of course as "unique," not as "an ordinary man," as Langdon supposes.

Line 236. On this title "wild cow of the stall" for Ninsun, see Poebel in *OLZ* 1914, page 6, to whom we owe the correct view regarding the name of Gilgamesh's mother.

Line 238. *mu-ti* here cannot mean "husband," but "man" in general. See above note to line 107. Langdon's strange misreading *ri-eš-su* for *ri-eš-ka* ("thy head") leads him again to miss the point, namely that Enkidu comforts his rival by telling him that he is destined for a career above that of the ordinary man. He is to be more than a mere prize fighter; he is to be a king, and no doubt in the ancient sense, as the representative of the deity. This is indicated by the statement that the kingship is decreed for him by Enlil. Similarly, Ḫu(m)baba or Ḫuwawa is designated by Enlil to inspire terror among men (Assyrian version, Tablet IV, 5, 2 and 5), *i-šim-šú* *dEnlil* = Yale tablet, l. 137, where this is to be supplied. This position accorded to Enlil is an important index for the origin of the Epic, which is thus shown to date from a period when the patron deity of Nippur was acknowledged as the general head of the pantheon. This justifies us in going back several centuries at least before Hammurabi for the beginning of the Gilgamesh story. If it had originated in the Hammurabi period, we should have had Marduk introduced instead of Enlil.

Line 242. As has been pointed out in the corrections to the text (Appendix), *šú-tu-ur* can only be III, 1, from *atâru*, "to be in excess of." It is a pity that the balance of the line is broken off, since this is the first instance of a colophon beginning with the term in question. In some way *šutûr* must indicate that the copy of the text has been "enlarged." It is tempting to fill out the line *šú-tu-ur e-li [duppi labiri]*, and to render "enlarged from an original," as an indication of an independent recension of the Epic in the Hammurabi period. All this, however, is purely conjectural, and we must patiently hope for more tablets of the Old Babylonian version to turn up. The chances are that some portions of the same edition as the Yale and Pennsylvania tablets are in the hands of dealers at present or have been sold to European museums. The war has seriously interfered with the possibility of tracing the whereabouts of groups of tablets that ought never to have been separated.

Yale Tablet

Transliteration.

(About ten lines missing.)

Col. I.

11................. [ib]-ri(?)

12[mi-im-ma(?) šá(?)]-kú-tu wa(?)-ak-rum

13[am-mi-nim] ta-aḫ-ši-iḫ

14[an-ni]-a-am [e-pi]-šá-am

15...... mi-im[-ma šá-kú-tu(?)]ma-

16di-iš

17[am-mi]-nim [taḫ]-ši-iḫ

18[ur(?)]-ta-du-ú [a-na ki-i]š-tim

19ši-ip-ra-am it-[ta-šú]-ú i-na [nišê]

20it-ta-áš-šú-ú-ma

21i-pu-šú ru-ḫu-tam

22................. uš-ta-di-nu

23............................ bu

24.............................

(About 17 lines missing.)

40............. nam-........

41................... u ib-[ri] .....

42............. ú-na-i-du ......

43[zi-ik]-ra-am ú-[tí-ir]-ru

44[a-na] ḫa-ri-[im]-tim

45[i]-pu(?)-šú a-na sa-[ka]-pu-ti

Col. II.

(About eleven lines missing.)

57... šú(?)-mu(?) ....

58ma-ḫi-ra-am [šá i-ši-šú]

59šú-uk-ni-šum-[ma] ....

60la-al-la-ru-[tu] ....

61um-mi ^{d}-[Giš mu-di-a-at ka-la-ma]

62i-na ma-[ḫar ^{d}Šamaš i-di-šá iš-ši]

63šá ú

64i-na- an(?)-[na am-mi-nim]

65ta-[aš-kun(?) a-na ma-ri-ia li-ib-bi la]

66ṣa-[li-la te-mid-su]

67............................

(About four lines missing.)

72i-na [šá ^{d}En-ki-dũ im-la-a] di-[im-tam]

73il-[pu-ut li]-ib-ba-šú-[ma]

74[zar-biš(?)] uš-ta-ni-[iḫ]

75[i-na šá ^{d}En]-ki-dũ im-la-a di-im-tam

76[il-pu-ut] li-ib-ba-šú-ma

77[zar-biš(?)] uš-ta-ni-[iḫ]

78[^{d}Giš ú-ta]-ab-bil pa-ni-šú

79[iz-za-kar-am] a-na ^{d}En-ki-dũ

80[ib-ri am-mi-nim] i-na-ka

81[im-la-a di-im]-tam

82[il-pu-ut li-ib-bi]-ka

83[zar-biš tu-uš-ta]-ni-iḫ

84[^{d}En-ki-dũ pi-šú i-pu-šá]-am-ma

85iz-za-[kàr-am] a-na ^{d}Giš

86ta-ab-bi-a-tum ib-ri

87uš-ta-li-pa da-1da-ni-ia

88a-ḫa-a-a ir-ma-a-ma

89e-mu-ki i-ni-iš

90^{d}Giš pi-šú i-pu-šá-am-ma

91iz-za-kàr-am a-na ^{d}En-ki-dũ

(About four lines missing.)

Col. III.

96..... [a-di ^{d}Ḫu]-wa-wa da-pi-nu

97................. ra-[am(?)-ma]

98............... [ú-ḫal]- li-ik

99[lu-ur-ra-du a-na ki-iš-ti šá] ^{is}erini

100........... lam(?) ḫal-bu

101........... [li]-li-is-su

102............. lu(?)-up-ti-šú

103^{d}En-ki-dũ pi-šú i-pu-šá-am-ma

104iz-za-kàr-am a-na ^{d}Giš

105i-di-ma ib-ri i-na šadî(-i)

106i-nu-ma at-ta-la-ku it-ti bu-lim

107a-na ištên(-en) kas-gíd-ta-a-an nu-ma-at ki-iš-tum

108[e-di-iš(?)] ur-ra-du a-na libbi-šá

109^{d}[Ḫu-wa]-wa ri-ig-ma-šú a-bu-bu

110pi-[šú] ^{d}Bil-gi-ma

111na-pi-iš-šú mu-tum

112am-mi-nim ta-aḫ-ši-iḫ

113an-ni-a-am e-pi-šá-am

114ga-[ba]-al-la ma-ḫa-ar

115[šú]-pa-at ^{d}Ḫu-wa-wa

116(^{d})Giš pi-šú i-pu-šá-am-ma

117[iz-za-k]àr-am a-na ^{d}En-ki-dũ

118....... su(?)-lu-li a-šá-ki2-šá

119............ [i-na ki-iš]-tim

120.............................

121ik(?) ....

122a-na ....

123mu-šá-ab [^{d}Ḫu-wa-wa] ....

124ḫa-aṣ-si-nu ....

125at-ta lu(?) ....

126a-na-ku lu-[ur-ra-du a-na ki-iš-tim]

127^{d}En-ki-dũ pi-šú i-pu-[šá-am-ma]

128iz-za-kàr-am a-na [^{d}Giš]

129ki-i ni[il]-la-ak [iš-te-niš(?)]

130a-na ki-iš-ti [šá ^{iṣ}erini]

131na-ṣi-ir-šá ^{d}Giš muḳ-[tab-lu]

132da-a-an la ṣa[-li-lu(?)]

133^{d}Ḫu-wa-wa ^{d}pi-ir-[ḫu ša (?)]

134^{d}Adad iš ....

135šú-ú ....

Col. IV.

136áš-šúm šú-ul-lu-m[u ki-iš-ti šá^{iṣ}erini]

137pu-ul-ḫi-a-tim 7 [šú(?) i-šim-šú ^{d}Enlil]

138^{d}Giš pi-šú i-pu [šá-am-ma]

139iz-za-kàr-am a-na [^{d}En-ki-dũ]

140ma-an-nu ib-ri e-lu-ú šá-[ru-ba(?)]

141i-ṭib-ma it-ti ^{d}Šamaš da-ri-iš ú-[me-šú]

142a-we-lu-tum ba-ba-nu ú-tam-mu-šá-[ma]

143mi-im-ma šá i-te-ni-pu-šú šá-ru-ba

144at-ta an-na-nu-um-ma ta-dar mu-tam

145ul iš-šú da-na-nu ḳar-ra-du-ti-ka

146lu-ul-li-ik-ma i-na pa-ni-ka

147pi-ka li-iš-si-a-am ṭi-ḫi-e ta-du-ur

148šum-ma am-ta-ḳu-ut šú-mi lu-uš-zi-iz

149^{d}Giš mi3-it-ti ^{d}Ḫu-wa-wa da-pi-nim

150il(?)-ḳu-ut iš-tu

151i-wa-al-dam-ma tar-bi-a i-na šam-mu(?) Il(?)

152iš-ḫi-it-ka-ma la-bu ka-la-ma ti-di

153it- ku(?) ..... [il(?)]-pu-tu-(?) ma .....

154............. ka-ma

155............. ši pi-ti

156............ ki-ma re'i(?) na-gi-la sa-rak-ti

157.... [ta-šá-s]i-a-am tu-lim-mi-in li-ib-bi

158[ga-ti lu]-uš-ku-un-ma

159[lu-u-ri]-ba-am ^{iṣ}erini

160[šú-ma sá]-ṭa-ru-ú a-na-ku lu-uš-ta-ak-na

161[pu-tu-ku(?)] ib-ri a-na ki-iš-ka-tim lu-mu-ḫa

162[be-le-e li-iš-]-pu-ku i-na maḫ-ri-ni

163[pu-tu]-ku a-na ki-iš-ka-ti-i i-mu-ḫu

164wa-áš-bu uš-ta-da-nu um-mi-a-nu

165pa-ši iš-pu-ku ra-bu-tim

166ḫa-aṣ-si-ni 3 biltu-ta-a-an iš-tap-ku

167pa-aṭ-ri iš-pu-ku ra-bu-tim

168me-še-li-tum 2 biltu-ta-a-an

169ṣi-ip-ru 30 ma-na-ta-a-an šá a-ḫi-ši-na

170išid(?) pa-aṭ-ri 30 ma-na-ta-a-an ḫuraṣi

171[^{d}]Giš ù [^{d}En-ki-]dũ 10 biltu-ta-a-an šá-ak-nu]

172.... ul-la . .[Uruk]^{ki} 7 i-di-il-šú

173...... iš-me-ma um-ma-nu ib-bi-ra

174[uš-te-(?)]-mi-a i-na sûḳi šá Uruk^{ki} ri-bi-tim

175...... [u-še(?)]-ṣa-šú ^{d}Gis

176[ina sûḳi šá(?) Uruk^{ki}] ri-bi-tim

177[^{d}En-ki-dũ(?) ú]-šá-ab i-na maḫ-ri-šú

178..... [ki-a-am(?) i-ga]-ab-bi

179[........ Uruk^{ki} ri]-bi-tim

180 [ma-ḫa-ar-šú]

Col. V.

181^{d}Giš šá i-ga-ab-bu-ú lu-mu-ur

182šá šú-um-šú it-ta-nam-ma-la ma-ta-tum

183lu-uk-šú-su-ma i-na ki-iš-ti ^{iṣ}erini

184ki-ma da-an-nu pi-ir-ḫu-um šá Uruk^{ki}

185lu-ši-eš-mi ma-tam

186ga-ti lu-uš-ku-un-ma lu-uk-[šú]4-su-ma ^{iṣ}erini

187šú-ma šá-ṭa-ru-ú a-na-ku lu-uš-tak-nam

188ši-bu-tum šá Uruk^{ki} ri-bi-tim

189zi-ik-ra ú-ti-ir-ru a-na ^{d}Giš

190ṣi-iḫ-ri-ti-ma ^{d}Giš libbi-ka na-ši-ka

191mi-im-ma šá te-te-ni-pu-šú la ti-di

192ni-ši-im-me-ma ^{d}Ḫu-wa-wa šá-nu-ú bu-nu-šú

193ma-an-nu-um [uš-tam]-ḫa-ru ka-ak-ki-šú

194a-na ištên(-en) [kas-gíd-ta-a]-an nu-ma-at kišti

195ma-an-nu šá [ur-ra]-du a-na libbi-šá

196^{d}Ḫu-wa-wa ri-ig-ma-šú a-bu-bu

197pi-šú ^{d}Bil-gi-ma na-pi-su mu-tum

198am-mi-nim taḫ-ši-iḫ an-ni-a-am e-pi-šá

199ga-ba-al-la ma-ḫa-ar šú-pa-at ^{d}Ḫu-wa-wa

200iš-me-e-ma ^{d}Giš zi-ki-ir ma-li-[ki]-šú

201ip-pa-al-sa-am-ma i-ṣi-iḫ a-na ib-[ri-šú]

202i-na-an-na ib-[ri] ki-a-am [a-ga-ab-bi]

203a-pa-al-aḫ-šú-ma a-[al-la-ak a-na kišti]

204[lu]ul-[lik it-ti-ka a-na ki-iš-ti ^{iṣ}erini(?)]

(About five lines missing.)

210........................ -ma

211li .... -ka

212ilu-ka li(?) ....-ka

213ḫarrana li-šá-[tir-ka a-na šú-ul-mi]

214a-na kar šá [Uruk^{ki} ri-bi-tim]

215ka-mi-is-ma ^{d}Giš [ma-ḫa-ar ^{d}Šamaš(?)]

216a-wa-at i-ga-ab- [bu-šú-ma]

217a-al-la-ak ^{d}Šamaš katâ-[ka a-ṣa-bat]

218ul-la-nu lu-uš-li-ma na-pi-[iš-ti]

219te-ir-ra-an-ni a-na kar i-[na Uruk^{ki}]

220ṣi-il-[la]m šú-ku-un [a-na ia-a-ši(?)]

221iš-si-ma ^{d}Giš ib-[ri.....]

222te-ir-ta-šú ....

223is(?) ....

224tam ....

225.......................

226i-nu(?)-[ma] ....

(About two lines missing.)

Col. VI.

229[a-na-ku] ^{d}Giš [i-ik]-ka-di ma-tum

230........... ḫarrana šá la al-[kam] ma-ti-ma

231.... a-ka-lu ..... la(?) i-di

232[ul-la-nu] lu-uš-li-[mu] a-na-ku

233[lu-ud-lul]-ka i-na [ḫ]u-ud li-ib-bi

234...... [šú]-ḳu-ut-[ti] la-li-ka

235[lu-še-šib(?)] - ka i-na kussê^{meš}

236...................... ú-nu-su

237[bêlê^{meš}(?)ú-ti-ir]-ru ra-bu-tum

238[ka-aš-tum] ù iš-pa-tum

239[i-na] ga-ti iš-ku-nu

240[il-]te-ki pa-ši

241....... -ri iš-pa-as-su

242..... [a-na] ili šá-ni-tam

243[it-ti pa(?)] - tar-[šú] i-na ši-ip-pi-šú

244........ i-ip-pu-šú a-la-kam

245[ša]-niš ú-ga-ra-bu ^{d}Giš

246[a-di ma]-ti tu-ut-te-ir a-na libbi Uruk^{ki}

247[ši-bu]-tum i-ka-ra-bu-šú

248[a-na] ḫarrani i-ma-li-ku ^{d}Giš

249[la t]a-at-kal ^{d}Giš a-na e-[mu]-ḳi-ka

250[a-]ka-lu šú-wa-ra-ma ú-ṣur ra-ma-an-ka

251[li]-il-lik ^{d}En-ki-dũ i-na pa-ni-ka

252[ur-ḫa]-am a-we-ir a-lik ḫarrana(-na)

253[a-di] šá kišti ni-ri-bi-tim

254[šá(?)] [^{d}]Ḫu-wa-wa ka-li-šú-nu ši-ip-pi-iḫ(?)-šú

255[ša(?)a-lik] maḫ-ra tap-pa-a ú-šá-lim

256[ḫarrana](-na)-šú šú-wa-ra-[ma ú-ṣur ra-ma-na-ka]

257[li-šak-šid]-ka ir-[ni-ta]-ka ^{d}Šamaš

258ta-ak-bi-a-at pi-ka li-kal-li-ma i-na-ka

259li-ip-ti-ḳu pa-da-nam pi-ḫi-tam

260ḫarrana li-iš-ta-zi-ik a-na ki-ib-si-ka

261šá-di-a li-iš-ta-zi-ik a-na šêpi-ka

262mu-ši-it-ka aw-a-at ta-ḫa-du-ú

263li-ib-la-ma ^{d}Lugal-ban-da li-iz-zi-iz-ka

264i-na ir-ni-ti-ka

265ki-ma ṣi-iḫ-ri ir-ni-ta-ka-ma luš-mida(-da)

266i-na na-ri šá ^{d}Ḫu-wa-wa šá tu-ṣa-ma-ru

267mi-zi ši-pi-ka

268i-na bat-ba-ti-ka ḫi-ri bu-ur-tam

269lu-ka-a-a-nu mê ellu i-na na-di-ka

270[ka-]su-tim me-e a-na ^{d}Šamaš ta-na-di

271[li-iš]ta-ḫa-sa-as ^{d}Lugal-ban-da

272[^{d}En-ki-]dũ pi-su i-pu-šá-am-ma, iz-za-kàr a-na ^{d}Giš

273[is(?)]-tu(?) ta-áš-dan-nu e-pu-uš a-la-kam

274[la pa]la-aḫ libbi-ka ia-ti tu-uk-la-ni

275[šú-ku-]un i-di-a-am šú-pa-as-su

276[ḫarrana(?)]šá ^{d}Ḫu-wa-wa it-ta-la-ku

277.......... ki-bi-ma te-[ir]-šú-nu-ti

(Three lines missing.)

L.E.

281.............. nam-ma-la

282............... il-li-ku it-ti-ia

283.............. ba-ku-nu-ši-im

284......... [ul]-la(?)-nu i-na ḫu-ud li-ib-bi

285[i-na še-me-e] an-ni-a ga-ba-šú

286e-diš ḫarrana(?) uš-te-[zi-ik]

287a-lik ^{d}Giš lu-[ul-lik a-na pa-ni-ka]

288li-lik il-ka ....

289li-šá-ak-lim-[ka ḫarrana] ......

290^{d}Giš ù[^{d}En-ki-dũ] ....

291mu-di-eš ....

292bi-ri-[su-nu] ....

Translation.

(About ten lines missing.)

Col. I.

11.................. (my friend?)

12[Something] that is exceedingly difficult,

13[Why] dost thou desire

14[to do this?]

15.... something (?) that is very [difficult (?)],

16[Why dost thou] desire

17[to go down to the forest]?

18A message [they carried] among [men]

19They carried about.

20They made a ....

21.............. they brought

22..............................

23..............................

(About 17 lines missing.)

40..............................

41................... my friend

42................ they raised .....

43answer [they returned.]

44[To] the woman

45They proceeded to the overthrowing

Col. II.

(About eleven lines missing.)

57.......... name(?) ....

58[The one who is] a rival [to him]

59subdue and ....

60Wailing ....

61The mother [of Gišh, who knows everything]

62Before [Shamash raised her hand]

63Who

64Now(?) [why]

65hast thou stirred up the heart for my son,

66[Restlessness imposed upon him (?)]

67............................

(About four lines missing.)

72The eyes [of Enkidu filled with tears].

73[He clutched] his heart;

74[Sadly(?)] he sighed.

75[The eyes of En]kidu filled with tears.

76[He clutched] his heart;

77[Sadly(?)] he sighed.

78The face [of Gišh was grieved].

79[He spoke] to Enkidu:

80[“My friend, why are] thy eyes

81[Filled with tears]?

82Thy [heart clutched]

83Dost thou sigh [sadly(?)]?”

84[Enkidu opened his mouth] and

85spoke to Gišh:

86“Attacks, my friend,

87have exhausted my strength(?).

88My arms are lame,

89my strength has become weak.”

90Gišh opened his mouth and

91spoke to Enkidu:

(About four lines missing.)

Col. III.

96..... [until] Ḫuwawa, [the terrible],

97........................

98............ [I destroyed].

99[I will go down to the] cedar forest,

100.................. the jungle

101............... tambourine (?)

102............... I will open it.

103Enkidu opened his mouth and

104spoke to Gišh:

105"Know, my friend, in the mountain,

106when I moved about with the cattle

107to a distance of one double hour into the heart of the forest,

108[Alone?] I penetrated within it,

109[To] Ḫuwawa, whose roar is a flood,

110whose mouth is fire,

111whose breath is death.

112Why dost thou desire

113To do this?

114To advance towards

115the dwelling(?) of Ḫuwawa?"

116Gišh opened his mouth and

117[spoke to Enkidu:

118"... [the covering(?)] I will destroy.

119....[in the forest]

120...................

121...................

122To ....

123The dwelling [of Ḫuwawa]

124The axe ....

125Thou ....

126I will [go down to the forest]."

127Enkidu opened his mouth and

128spoke to [Gish:]

129“When [together(?)] we go down

130To the [cedar] forest,

131whose guardian, O warrior Gish,

132a power(?) without [rest(?)],

133Ḫuwawa, an offspring(?) of ....

134Adad ....

135He ....

Col. IV.

136To keep safe [the cedar forest],

137[Enlil has decreed for it] seven-fold terror.”

138Gish [opened] his mouth and

139spoke to [Enkidu]:

140“Whoever, my friend, overcomes (?) [terror(?)],

141it is well (for him) with Shamash for the length of [his days].

142Mankind will speak of it at the gates.

143Wherever terror is to be faced,

144Thou, forsooth, art in fear of death.

145Thy prowess lacks strength.

146I will go before thee.

147Though thy mouth calls to me; “thou art afraid to approach.”

148If I fall, I will establish my name.

149Gish, the corpse(?) of Ḫuwawa, the terrible one,

150has snatched (?) from the time that

151My offspring was born in ......

152The lion restrained (?) thee, all of which thou knowest.

153.......................

154............. thee and

155................ open (?)

156........ like a shepherd(?) .....

157[When thou callest to me], thou afflictest my heart.

158I am determined

159[to enter] the cedar forest.

160I will, indeed, establish my name.

161[The work(?)], my friend, to the artisans I will entrust.

162[Weapons(?)] let them mould before us."

163[The work(?)] to the artisans they entrusted.

164A dwelling(?) they assigned to the workmen.

165Hatchets the masters moulded:

166Axes of 3 talents each they moulded.

167Lances the masters moulded;

168Blades(?) of 2 talents each,

169A spear of 30 mina each attached to them.

170The hilt of the lances of 30 mina in gold

171Gish and [Enki]du were equipped with 10 talents each

172.......... in Erech seven its ....

173....... the people heard and ....

174[proclaimed(?)] in the street of Erech of the plazas.

175..... Gis [brought him out(?)]

176[In the street (?)] of Erech of the plazas

177[Enkidu(?)] sat before him

178..... [thus] he spoke:

179"........ [of Erech] of the plazas

180............ [before him]

Col. V.

181Gish of whom they speak, let me see!

182whose name fills the lands.

183I will lure him to the cedar forest,

184Like a strong offspring of Erech.

185I will let the land hear (that)

186I am determined to lure (him) in the cedar (forest)[5].

187A name I will establish."

188The elders of Erech of the plazas

189brought word to Gish:

190"Thou art young, O Gish, and thy heart carries thee away.

191Thou dost not know what thou proposest to do.

192We hear that Huwawa is enraged.

193Who has ever opposed his weapon?

194To one [double hour] in the heart of the forest,

195Who has ever penetrated into it?

196Ḫuwawa, whose roar is a deluge,

197whose mouth is fire, whose breath is death.

198Why dost thou desire to do this?

199To advance towards the dwelling (?) of Ḫuwawa?"

200Gish heard the report of his counsellors.

201He saw and cried out to [his] friend:

202"Now, my friend, thus [I speak].

203I fear him, but [I will go to the cedar forest(?)];

204I will go [with thee to the cedar forest].

(About five lines missing.)

210............................

211May .... thee

212Thy god may (?) .... thee;

213On the road may he guide [thee in safety(?)].

214At the rampart of [Erech of the plazas],

215Gish kneeled down [before Shamash(?)],

216A word then he spoke [to him]:

217"I will go, O Shamash, [thy] hands [I seize hold of].

218When I shall have saved [my life],

219Bring me back to the rampart [in Erech].

220Grant protection [to me ?]!"

221Gish cried, "[my friend] ......

222His oracle ....

223.......................

224.......................

225.......................

226When (?)

(About two lines missing.)

Col. VI.

229"[I(?)] Gish, the strong one (?) of the land.

230...... A road which I have never [trodden];

231........ food ...... do not (?) know.

232[When] I shall have succeeded,

233[I will praise] thee in the joy of my heart,

234[I will extol (?)] the superiority of thy power,

235[I will seat thee] on thrones."

236................. his vessel(?)

237The masters [brought the weapons (?)];

238[bow] and quiver

239They placed in hand.

240[He took] the hatchet.

241................. his quiver.

242..... [to] the god(?) a second time

243[With his lance(?)] in his girdle,

244......... they took the road.

245[Again] they approached Gish!

246"[How long] till thou returnest to Erech?"

247[Again the elders] approached him.

248[For] the road they counselled Gis:

249"Do [not] rely, O Gish, on thy strength!

250Provide food and save thyself!

251Let Enkidu go before thee.

252He is acquainted with the way, he has trodden the road

253[to] the entrance of the forest.

254of Ḫuwawa all of them his ......

255[He who goes] in advance will save the companion.

256Provide for his [road] and [save thyself]!

257(May) Shamash [carry out] thy endeavor!

258May he make thy eyes see the prophecy of thy mouth.

259May he track out (for thee) the closed path!

260May he level the road for thy treading!

261May he level the mountain for thy foot!

262During thy night6 the word that wilt rejoice

263may Lugal-banda convey, and stand by thee

264in thy endeavor!

265Like a youth may he establish thy endeavor!

266In the river of Ḫuwawa as thou plannest,

267wash thy feet!

268Round about thee dig a well!

269May there be pure water constantly for thy libation

270Goblets of water pour out to Shamash!

271[May] Lugal-banda take note of it!"

272[Enkidu] opened his mouth and spoke to Gish:

273"[Since thou art resolved] to take the road.

274Thy heart [be not afraid,] trust to me!

275[Confide] to my hand his dwelling(?)!"

276[on the road to] Ḫuwawa they proceeded.

277....... command their return

(Three lines missing.)

L.E.

281............... were filled.

282.......... they will go with me.

283...............................

284................. joyfully.

285[Upon hearing] this word of his,

286Alone, the road(?) [he levelled].

287"Go, O Gish [I will go before thee(?)].

288May thy god(?) go ....

289May he show [thee the road !] .....

290Gish and [Enkidu]

291Knowingly ....

292Between [them] ....

Lines 13–14 (also line 16). See for the restoration, lines 112–13.

Line 62. For the restoration, see Jensen, p. 146 (Tablet III, 2^a,9.)

Lines 64–66. Restored on the basis of the Assyrian version, *ib.* line 10.

Line 72. Cf. Assyrian version, Tablet IV, 4, 10, and restore at the end of this line *di-im-tam* as in our text, instead of Jensen's conjecture.

Lines 74, 77 and 83. The restoration *ẓar-biš*, suggested by the Assyrian version, Tablet IV, 4, 4.

Lines 76 and 82. Cf. Assyrian version, Tablet VIII, 3, 18.

Line 78. *(ú-ta-ab-bil* from *abâlu*, "grieve" or "darkened." Cf. *uš-ta-ḳal* (Assyrian version, *ib.* line 9), where, perhaps, we are to restore *it-ta-[bil pa-ni-šú]*.

Line 87. *uš-ta-li-pa* from *elêpu*, "exhaust." See Muss-Arnolt, *Assyrian Dictionary*, p. 49a.

Line 89. Cf. Assyrian version, *ib.* line 11, and restore the end of the line there to *i-ni-iš*, as in our text.

Line 96. For *dapinu* as an epithet of Ḫuwawa, see Assyrian version, Tablet III, 2a, 17, and 3a, 12. *Dapinu* occurs also as a description of an ox (Rm 618, Bezold, *Catalogue of the Kouyunjik Tablets*, etc., p. 1627).

Line 98. The restoration on the basis of *ib.* III, 2a, 18.

Lines 96–98 may possibly form a parallel to *ib.* lines 17–18, which would then read about as follows: "Until I overcome Ḫuwawa, the terrible, and all the evil in the land I shall have destroyed." At the same time, it is possible that we are to restore *[lu-ul]-li-ik* at the end of line 98.

Line 101. *lilissu* occurs in the Assyrian version, Tablet IV, 6, 36.

Line 100. For *ḫalbu*, "jungle," see Assyrian version, Tablet V, 3, 39 (p. 160).

Lines 109–111. These lines enable us properly to restore Assyrian version, Tablet IV, 5, 3 = Haupt's edition, p. 83 (col. 5, 3). No doubt the text read as ours *mu-tum* (or *mu-u-tum*) *na-pis-su*.

Line 115. *šupatu*, which occurs again in line 199 and also line 275.*šú-pa-as-su* (= *šupat-su*) must have some such meaning as "dwelling," demanded by the context. [Dhorme refers me to *OLZ* 1916, p. 145].

Line 129. Restored on the basis of the Assyrian version, Tablet IV, 6, 38.

Line 131. The restoration *muḳtablu*, tentatively suggested on the basis of CT XVIII, 30, 7b, where *muḳtablu*, "warrior," appears as one of the designations of Gilgamesh, followed by *a-lik pa-na*, "the one who goes in advance," or "leader"—the phrase so constantly used in the Ḫuwawa episode.

Line 132. Cf. Assyrian version, Tablet I, 5, 18–19.

Lines 136–137. These two lines restored on the basis of Jensen IV, 5, 2 and 5. The variant in the Assyrian version, *šá niše* (written Uku^{meš} in one case and Lu^{meš} in the other), for the numeral 7 in our text to designate a terror of the largest and most widespread character, is interesting. The number 7 is similarly used as a designation of Gilgamesh, who is called *Esigga imin*, "seven-fold strong," i.e., supremely strong (CT XVIII, 30, 6–8). Similarly, Enkidu, *ib.* line 10, is designated *a-rá imina*, "seven-fold."

Line 149. A difficult line because of the uncertainty of the reading at the beginning of the following line. The most obvious meaning of *mi-it-tu* is "corpse," though in the Assyrian version *šalamtu* is used (Assyrian version, Tablet V, 2, 42). On the other hand, it is possible—as Dr. Lutz suggested to me—that *mittu*, despite the manner of writing, is identical with *miṭṭú*, the name of a divine weapon, well-known from the Assyrian creation myth (Tablet IV, 130), and other passages. The combination *miṭ-ṭu šá-ḳu-ú-*, "lofty weapon," in the Bilingual text IV, R^2, 18 No. 3, 31–32, would favor the meaning "weapon" in our passage, since *[šá]-ḳu-tu* is a possible restoration at the beginning of line 150. However, the writing *mi-it-ti* points too distinctly to a derivative of the stem *mâtu*, and until a satisfactory explanation of lines 150–152 is forthcoming, we must stick to the meaning "corpse" and read the verb *il-ḳu-ut*.

Line 152. The context suggests "lion" for the puzzling *la-bu*.

Line 156. Another puzzling line. Dr. Clay's copy is an accurate reproduction of what is distinguishable. At the close of the line there appears to be a sign written over an erasure.

Line 158. *[ga-ti lu-]uš-kun* as in line 186, literally, "I will place my hand," i.e., I purpose, I am determined.

Line 160. The restoration on the basis of the parallel line 187. Note the interesting phrase, "writing a name" in the sense of acquiring "fame."

Line 161. The *kiškattê*, "artisans," are introduced also in the Assyrian version, Tablet VI, 187, to look at the enormous size and weight of the horns of the slain divine bull. See for other passages Muss-Arnolt *Assyrian Dictionary*, p. 450^{b}. At the beginning of this line, we must seek for the same word as in line 163.

Line 162. While the restoration *belê*, "weapon," is purely conjectural, the context clearly demands some such word. I choose *belê* in preference to *kakkê*, in view of the Assyrian version, Tablet VI, 1.

Line 163. *Putuku* (or *putukku*) from *patâku* would be an appropriate word for the fabrication of weapons.

Line 165. The *rabûtim* here, as in line 167, I take as the "master mechanics" as contrasted with the *ummianu*, "common workmen," or journeymen. A parallel to this forging of the weapons for the two heroes is to be found in the Sumerian fragment of the Gilgamesh Epic published by Langdon, *Historical and Religious Texts from the Temple Library of Nippur* (Munich, 1914), No. 55, 1–15.

Lines 168–170 describe the forging of the various parts of the lances for the two heroes. The *Ṣipru* is the spear point Muss-Arnolt, *Assyrian Dictionary*, p. 886^{b}; the *išid paṭri* is clearly the "hilt," and the *mešelitum* I therefore take as the "blade" proper. The word occurs here for the first time, so far as I can see. For 30 minas, see Assyrian version, Tablet VI, 189, as the weight of the two horns of the divine bull. Each axe weighing 3 *biltu*, and the lance with point and hilt 3 *biltu* we would have to assume 4 *biltu* for each *pašu*, so as to get a total of 10 *biltu* as the weight of the weapons for each hero. The lance is depicted on seal cylinders representing Gilgamesh and Enkidu, for example, Ward, *Seal Cylinders*, No. 199, and also in Nos. 184 and 191 in the field, with the broad hilt; and in an enlarged form in No. 648. Note the clear indication of the hilt. The two figures are Gilgamesh and Enkidu—not two Gilgameshes, as Ward assumed. See above, page 34. A different weapon is the club or mace, as seen in Ward, Nos. 170 and 173. This appears also to be the weapon which Gilgamesh holds in his hand on the colossal figure from the palace of Sargon (Jastrow, *Civilization of Babylonia and Assyria*, Pl. LVII), though it has been given a somewhat grotesque character by a perhaps intentional approach to the scimitar, associated with Marduk (see Ward, *Seal Cylinders*, Chap. XXVII). The exact determination of the various weapons depicted on seal-cylinders merits a special study.

Line 181. Begins a speech of Ḫuwawa, extending to line 187, reported to Gish by the elders (line 188–189), who add a further warning to the youthful and impetuous hero.

Line 183. *lu-uk-šú-su* (also l. 186), from *akâšu*, "drive on" or "lure on," occurs on the Pennsylvania tablet, line 135, *uk-ki-ši*, "lure on" or "entrap," which Langdon erroneously renders "take away" and thereby misses the point completely. See the comment to the line of the Pennsylvania tablet in question.

Line 192. On the phrase *šanû bunu*, "change of countenance," in the sense of "enraged," see the note to the Pennsylvania tablet, l.31.

Line 194. *nu-ma-at* occurs in a tablet published by Meissner, *Altbabyl. Privatrecht*, No. 100, with *bît abi*, which shows that the total confine of a property is meant; here, therefore, the "interior" of the forest or heart. It is hardly a "by-form" of *nuptum* as Muss-Arnolt, *Assyrian Dictionary*, p. 690[b], and others have supposed, though *nu-um-tum* in one passage quoted by Muss-Arnolt, *ib.* p. 705[a], may have arisen from an aspirate pronunciation of the *p* in *nubtum.*

Line 215. The kneeling attitude of prayer is an interesting touch. It symbolizes submission, as is shown by the description of Gilgamesh's defeat in the encounter with Enkidu (Pennsylvania tablet, l. 227), where Gilgamesh is represented as forced to "kneel" to the ground. Again in the Assyrian version, Tablet V, 4, 6, Gilgamesh kneels down (though the reading *ka-mis* is not certain) and has a vision.

Line 229. It is much to be regretted that this line is so badly preserved, for it would have enabled us definitely to restore the opening line of the Assyrian version of the Gilgamesh Epic. The fragment published by Jeremias in his appendix to his *Izdubar-Nimrod*, Plate IV, gives us the end of the colophon line to the Epic, reading .... *di ma-a-ti* (cf. *ib.*,

Pl. I, 1. … *a-ti*). Our text evidently reproduces the same phrase and enables us to supply *ka*, as well as the name of the hero Gišh of which there are distinct traces. The missing word, therefore, describes the hero as the ruler, or controller of the land. But what are the two signs before *ka*? A participial form from *pakâdu*, which one naturally thinks of, is impossible because of the *ka*, and for the same reason one cannot supply the word for shepherd (*nakidu*). One might think of *ka-ak-ka-du*, except that *kakkadu* is not used for "head" in the sense of "chief" of the land. I venture to restore *[i-ik-]ka-di*, "strong one." Our text at all events disposes of Haupt's conjecture *iš-di ma-a-ti* (*JAOS* 22, p. 11), "Bottom of the earth," as also of Ungnad's proposed *[a-di pa]-a-ti*, "to the ends" (Ungnad-Gressmann, *Gilgamesch-Epos*, p. 6, note), or a reading *di-ma-a-ti*, "pillars." The first line of the Assyrian version would now read

šá nak-ba i-mu-ru [dGis-gi(n)-maš i-ik-ka]-di ma-a-ti,

i.e., "The one who saw everything, Gilgamesh the strong one (?) of the land."

We may at all events be quite certain that the name of the hero occurred in the first line and that he was described by some epithet indicating his superior position.

Lines 229–235 are again an address of Gilgamesh to the sun-god, after having received a favorable "oracle" from the god (line 222). The hero promises to honor and to celebrate the god, by erecting thrones for him.

Lines 237–244 describe the arming of the hero by the "master" craftsman. In addition to the *pašu* and *paṭru*, the bow (?) and quiver are given to him.

Line 249 is paralleled in the new fragment of the Assyrian version published by King in *PSBA* 1914, page 66 (col. 1, 2), except that this fragment adds *gi-mir* to *e-mu-ḳi-ka*.

Lines 251–252 correspond to column 1, 6–8, of King's fragment, with interesting variations "battle" and "fight" instead of "way" and "road," which show that in the interval between the old Babylonian and the Assyrian version, the real reason why Enkidu should lead the way, namely, because he knows the country in which Ḫuwawa dwells (lines

252–253), was supplemented by describing Enkidu also as being more experienced in battle than Gilgamesh.

Line 254. I am unable to furnish a satisfactory rendering for this line, owing to the uncertainty of the word at the end. Can it be "his household," from the stem which in Hebrew gives us מִשְׁפָּחָה "family?"

Line 255. Is paralleled by col. 1, 4, of King's new fragment. The episode of Gišh and Enkidu proceeding to Ninsun, the mother of Gish, to obtain her counsel, which follows in King's fragment, appears to have been omitted in the old Babylonian version. Such an elaboration of the tale is exactly what we should expect as it passed down the ages.

Line 257. Our text shows that *irnittu* (lines 257, 264, 265) means primarily "endeavor," and then success in one's endeavor, or "triumph."

Lines 266–270. Do not appear to refer to rites performed after a victory, as might at a first glance appear, but merely voice the hope that Gišh will completely take possession of Ḫuwawa's territory, so as to wash up after the fight in Ḫuwawa's own stream; and the hope is also expressed that he may find pure water in Ḫuwawa's land in abundance, to offer a libation to Šhamašh.

Line 275. *On šú-pa-as-su = šupat-su*, see above, to l. 115.

[Note on Sabitum (above, p. 11)

In a communication before the Oriental Club of Philadelphia (Feb. 10, 1920), Prof. Haupt made the suggestion that *sa-bi-tum* (or *tu*), hitherto regarded as a proper name, is an epithet describing the woman who dwells at the seashore which Gilgamesh in the course of his wanderings reaches, as an "innkeeper". It is noticeable that the term always appears without the determinative placed before proper names; and since in the old Babylonian version (so far as preserved) and in the Assyrian version, the determinative is invariably used, its consistent absence in the case of *sabitum* (Assyrian Version, Tablet X, 1, 1, 10, 15, 20; 2, 15–16 [*sa-bit*]; Meissner fragment col. 2, 11–12) speaks in favor of Professor Haupt's suggestion. The meaning "innkeeper", while not as yet found in Babylonian-Assyrian literature is most plausible, since we have *sabū* as a general name for 'drink', though originally designating perhaps more specifically sesame wine (Muss-Arnolt, Assyrian

Dictionary, p. 745^{b}) or distilled brandy, according to Prof. Haupt. Similarly, in the Aramaic dialects, *s*^{e}*b*^{h}*a* is used for "to drink" and in the Pael to "furnish drink". Muss-Arnolt in his Assyrian Dictionary, 746^{b}, has also recognized that *sabitum* was originally an epithet and compares the Aramaic *s*^{e}*b*^{h}*oyâthâ*(p1) "barmaids". In view of the bad reputation of inns in ancient Babylonia as brothels, it would be natural for an epithet like *sabitum* to become the equivalent to "public" women, just as the inn was a "public" house. Sabitum would, therefore, have the same force as *šamḫatu* (the "harlot"), used in the Gilgamesh Epic by the side of *ḫarimtu* "woman" (see the note to line 46 of Pennsylvania Tablet). The Sumerian term for the female innkeeper is Sal Geštinna "the woman of the wine," known to us from the Hammurabi Code §§108–111. The bad reputation of inns is confirmed by these statutes, for the house of the Sal Geštinna is a gathering place for outlaws. The punishment of a female devotee who enters the "house of a wine woman" (bît Sal Geštinna §110) is death. It was not "prohibition" that prompted so severe a punishment, but the recognition of the purpose for which a devotee would enter such a house of ill repute. The speech of the *sabitum* or innkeeper to Gilgamesh (above, p. 12) was, therefore, an invitation to stay with her, instead of seeking for life elsewhere. Viewed as coming from a "public woman" the address becomes significant. The invitation would be parallel to the temptation offered by the *ḫarimtu* in the first tablet of the Enkidu, and to which Enkidu succumbs. The incident in the tablet would, therefore, form a parallel in the adventures of Gilgamesh to the one that originally belonged to the Enkidu cycle. Finally, it is quite possible that *sabitum* is actually the Akkadian equivalent of the Sumerian Sal Geštinna, though naturally until this equation is confirmed by a syllabary or by other direct evidence, it remains a conjecture. See now also Albright's remarks on Sabitum in the A. J. S. L. 36, pp. 269 *seq.*]

1 Scribal error for *an.*

2 Text apparently *di.*

3 Hardly *ul.*

4 Omitted by scribe.

5 *Kišti* omitted by scribe.

6 I.e., at night to thee, may Lugal-banda, etc.

Corrections to the Text of Langdon's Edition of the Pennsylvania Tablet.1

Column 1.

5. Read *it-lu-tim* ("heroes") instead of *id-da-tim* ("omens").

6. Read *ka-ka-bu* instead of *ka-ka-'a*. This disposes of Langdon's note 2 on p. 211.

9 Read *ú-ni-iš-šú-ma*, "I became weak" (from *enêšu*, "weak") instead of *ilam iš-šú-ma*, "He bore a net"(!). This disposes of Langdon's note 5 on page 211.

10. Read *Uruk*^{ki} instead of *ad-ki*. Langdon's note 7 is wrong.

12. Langdon's note 8 is wrong. *ú-um-mid-ma pu-ti* does not mean "he attained my front."

14. Read *ab-ba-la-áš-šú* instead of *at-ba-la-áš-šú*.

15. Read *mu-di-a-at* instead of *mu-u-da-a-at*.

20. Read *ta-ḫa-du* instead of an impossible *[sa]-ah-ḫa-ta*—two mistakes in one word. Supply *kima Sal* before *taḫadu*.

22. Read *áš-šú* instead of *šú*; and at the end of the line read *[tu-ut]-tu-ú-ma* instead of *šú-ú-zu*.

23. Read *ta-tar-ra-[as-su]*.

24. Read *[uš]-ti-nim-ma* instead of *[iš]-ti-lam-ma*.

28. Read at the beginning *šá* instead of *ina*.

29. Langdon's text and transliteration of the first word do not tally. Read *ḫa-aṣ-ṣi-nu*, just as in line 31.

32. Read *aḫ-ta-du* ("I rejoiced") instead of *aḫ-ta-ta*.

Column 2.

4. Read at the end of the line *di-da-šá(?) ip-tí-[e]* instead of *Di-?-al-lu-un* (!).

5. Supply ^{d}*En-ki-dū* at the beginning. Traces point to this reading.

19. Read *[gi]-it-ma-[lu]* after ^{d}*Giš*, as suggested by the Assyrian version, Tablet I, 4, 38, where *emûḳu* ("strength") replaces *nepištu* of our text.

20. Read *at-[ta kima Sal ta-ḫa]-bu-[ub]-šú.*

21. Read *ta-[ra-am-šú ki-ma]*.

23. Read as one word *ma-a-ag-ri-i-im* ("accursed"), spelled in characteristic Hammurabi fashion, instead of dividing into two words *ma-a-ak* and *ri-i-im*, as Langdon does, who suggests as a translation "unto the place yonder(?) of the shepherd"(!).

24. Read *im-ta-ḫar* instead of *im-ta-gar.*

32. Supply *ili*(?) after *ki-ma.*

33. Read *šá-ri-i-im* as one word.

35. Read *i-na [áš]-ri-šú [im]-ḫu-ru.*

36. Traces at beginning point to either *ù* or *ki* (= *itti*). Restoration of lines 36–39 (perhaps to be distributed into five lines) on the basis of the Assyrian version, Tablet I, 4, 2–5.

Column 3.

14. Read *Kàš* (= *šikaram*, "wine") *ši-ti*, "drink," as in line 17, instead of *bi-iš-ti*, which leads Langdon to render this perfectly simple line "of the conditions and the fate of the land"(!).

21. Read *it-tam-ru* instead of *it-ta-bir-ru.*

22. Supply *[*^{lù}*Šú]-I.*

29. Read *ú-gi-ir-ri* from *garû* ("attack), instead of separating into *ú* and *gi-ir-ri*, as Langdon does, who translates "and the lion." The sign used can *never* stand for the copula! Nor is *girru*, "lion!"

30. Read *Síb*^{meš}, "shepherds," instead of *šab-[ši]-eš*!

31. *šib-ba-ri* is not "mountain goat," nor can *ut-tap-pi-iš* mean "capture." The first word means "dagger," and the second "he drew out."

33. Read *it-ti-[lu] na-ki-[di-e]*, instead of *itti immer nakie* which yields no sense. Langdon's rendering, even on the basis of his reading of the line, is a grammatical monstrosity.

35. Read *giš* instead of *wa.*

37. Read perhaps *a-na [na-ki-di-e i]- za-ak-ki-ir.*

Column 4.

4. The first sign is clearly *iz*, not *ta*, as Langdon has it in note 1 on page 216.

9. The fourth sign is *su*, not *šú*.

10. Separate *e-eš* ("why") from the following. Read *ta-ḫi-[il]*, followed, perhaps, by *la*. The last sign is not certain; it may be *ma*.

11. Read *lim-nu* instead of *mi-nu*. In the same line read *a-la-ku ma-na-aḫ-[ti]-ka* instead of *a-la-ku-zu*(!) *na-aḫ ... ma*, which, naturally, Langdon cannot translate.

16. Read *e-lu-tim* instead of *pa-a-ta-tim*. The first sign of the line, *tu*, is not certain, because apparently written over an erasure. The second sign may be *a*. Some one has scratched the tablet at this point.

18. Read *uk-la-at âli* (?) instead of *ug-ad-ad-lil*, which gives no possible sense!

Column 5.

2. Read *[wa]-ar-ki-šú.*

8. Read *i-ta-wa-a* instead of *i-ta-me-a*. The word *pi-it-tam* belongs to line 9! The sign *pi* is unmistakable. This disposes of note 1 on p. 218.

9. Read Mi = *Ṣalmu*, "image." This disposes of Langdon's note 2 on page 218. Of six notes on this page, four are wrong.

11. The first sign appears to be *si* and the second *ma*. At the end we are perhaps to supply *[šá-ki-i pu]-uk-ku-ul*, on the basis of the Assyrian version, Tablet IV, 2, 45, *šá-ki-i pu-[uk-ku-ul]*.

12. Traces at end of line suggest *i-pa(?)-ka-du*.

13. Read *i-[na mâti da-an e-mu]-ki i-wa.*

18. Read *ur-šá-nu* instead of *ip-šá-nu*.

19. Read *i-šá-ru* instead of *i-tu-ru*.

24. The reading *it-ti* after *ᵈGiš* is suggested by the traces.

25. Read *in-ni-[ib-bi-it]* at the end of the line.

28. Read *ip-ta-ra-[aṣ a-la]-ak-tam* at the end of the line, as in the Assyrian version, Tablet IV, 2, 37.

30. The conjectural restoration is based on the Assyrian version, Tablet IV, 2, 36.

Column 6.

3. Read *i-na ṣi-ri-[šú]*.

5. Supply *[il-li-ik]*.

21. Langdon's text has a superfluous *ga*.

22. Read *uz-za-šú*, "his anger," instead of *uṣ-ṣa-šú*, "his javelin" (!).

23. Read *i-ni-iḫ i-ra-as-su*, i.e., "his breast was quieted," in the sense of "his anger was appeased."

31. Read *ri-eš-ka* instead of *ri-eš-su*.

In general, it should be noted that the indications of the number of lines missing at the bottom of columns 1–3 and at the top of columns 4–6 as given by Langdon are misleading. Nor should he have drawn any lines at the bottom of columns 1–3 as though the tablet were complete. Besides in very many cases the space indications of what is missing within a line are inaccurate. Dr. Langdon also omitted to copy the statement on the edge: *4 šú-ši*, i.e., "240 lines;" and in the colophon he mistranslates *šú-tu-ur*, "written," as though from *šaṭâru*, "write," whereas the form is the permansive III, 1, of *atâru*, "to be in excess of." The sign *tu* never has the value *ṭu*! In all, Langdon has misread the text or mistransliterated it in over forty places, and of the 204 preserved lines he has mistranslated about one-half.

1 The enumeration here is according to Langdon's edition.

TABLETS

TABLET I

Of this tablet only a few fragments are preserved. The correct beginning of the first tablet has been determined by Professor Haupt. It reads thus:

He who has seen the history of Gilgamesh,

[He who] knows all [that has happened to him]

* * * together * * *

[He who] has seen all kinds of wisdom,

[and] knows the mysteries and has seen what is hidden,

he bringeth news dating farther back [than the deluge?];

He has travelled far-distant roads,

and become weary * * *

[and now he has written] on a memorial tablet all the other things

* * * the wall of Uruk-supuru

[Lines ten and eleven are wanting.]

He spoke a charm which does not leave [him]

* * * the god who from distant days * * *

So far page 1 of Haupt's text; to the same tablet, as Haupt and Jeremias have pointed out, belongs page 51, narrating a siege of the city of Erech.

* * * his cattle forsook him.

* * * he went down to the river,

pushed into the river his boat and covered (it).

* * * full of sorrows he wept bitterly.

He returned (?) to the city of Gan-gan-na, which the enemy had destroyed completely.

The she-asses have trampled down their foals;

The cows in madness turn upon their calves.

And as the cattle were frightened, so were the people.

Like the doves, the maidens sigh and mourn.

The gods of Uruk, the strong-walled,

Assume the shape of flies and buzz about the streets.

The protecting deities of Uruk, the strong-walled,

take on the shape of mice and hurry into their holes.

Three years the enemy besieged the city of Uruk;

the city's gates were barred, the bolts were shot.

And even Ishtar, the goddess, could not make head against the enemy.

But Bel opened his mouth, said

to Ishtar, the queen, and spoke to her thus:

[The rest of the text is broken off; traces still allow to read (21) "Babylon the city of joy" (?). The death of the king must have created consternation in the city, described above, so graphically. Then Gilgamesh comes to the city as her saviour, and later on appears as her king.]

TABLET II

With the exception of Column I the text of this tablet is preserved almost completely. Gilgamesh is introduced as the ruler of Uruk, but his rule soon became unpopular, since he compelled all the young men of the city to enter his service, and carried off the maidens to his court. The parents complained, saying:

Not does Gilgamesh leave the son to his father,

nor the maiden to the warrior, nor the wife to her husband.

Their wailing and lament [is heard everywhere?].

"Ye gods of heaven, and thou Bel of Uruk,

who didst bring my son into existence, [save us!?],

He (Gilgamesh) has not a rival [in all the land?]

Thy people now come [to thee for help?].

Gilgamesh leaves not to the father his child." Day and night [they poured out their plaint]:

"He the ruler of Uruk the strong-walled.

He their ruler and

the strong, the lofty, the cunning [* * *]

Gilgamesh does not leave a daughter to [her mother?]

nor the maiden to the warrior, nor the wife to her husband."

[The gods of heaven] heard their cry.

They also cried aloud to Aruru, the goddess, saying: "Aruru, who hast created him,

Create now a rival (?) to him, for the time when his heart shall be [* * *],

Let them fight together and Uruk [shall be the spectator?]!"

Upon hearing this Aruru created in her heart a man after the likeness of Anu.

Aruru washed her hands, took a bit of clay, and cast it on the ground.

Thus she created Enkidu, the hero, a lofty offspring, the possession (?) of Ninib.

His whole body was covered with hair; he had long hair on his head Tike a woman;

His flowing hair was luxuriant like that of the corn-god.

Contrary to [?] the custom of the people and of the land, he was clothed with garments, as god Ner;

He ate herbs with the gazelles.

He quenched his thirst with the beasts.

He sported about with the creatures of the water.

Sa-a-a-du, the hunter of men.

Lay in wait for him at the entrance to the well.

The first, the second, and the third day he lay in wait for

him at the entrance to the well.

But when he saw him the hunter's face looked troubled,

[beholding Enkidu and?] his cattle, and he returned to his home.

* * * he was sad, and moaned, and wailed;

his heart grew heavy], his face became clouded,

and sadness [entered] into his mind.

His face became like unto [the distant * * * (?)]

The hunter, obeying the command of Gilgamesh, intended to advance against Enkidu; but at the sight of him he drew back in fear, and was unable to catch him.

The hunter opened his mouth and said unto [Ea, or Shamash, his father?]:

"My father, one hero, going there [is not strong enough?].

In heaven is * * *

Like that of a Kisir Anuis his strength;

he roams over [all] the mountains;

with the beasts of the field he regularly [feeds].

His feet are regularly set toward the entrance of the well.

I am afraid of him, I do not dare to go near him.

He has filled up the pit that I digged,

and has destroyed the hunter's nets which I [had spread over it?].

From my hands he has made to escape the cattle and the beasts of the field,

and does not allow me to hunt them."

His father opened his mouth and] spoke thus to the hunter:

["Go and wend thy way] to Uruk, the city of Gilgamesh.

The fragments of lines following show that the hunter was to find there a tempter called Shamhat, in order to entice, with her assistance, the sensuous Enkidu, and bring him to Uruk. Obeying the advice of his father, the hunter goes to Uruk [the city of Gilgamesh].

Into the presence] of Gilgamesh [stepped the hunter, and said:]

And now follows a repetition of the same report of the hunter concerning his failure to capture Enkidu, the address "my father," of course, being omitted. Thereupon:

Gilgamesh spoke to the hunter and said:

"Go, hunter mine, and take the ensnarer Shamhat with thee.

And when the beasts come down to the well,

then let her tear off her dress and disclose her nakedness.

Enkidu will see her, and he shall approach unto her,

and the cattle, which gather around him on the field, shall forsake him."

The hunter departed, and took with him the woman Shamhat.

Together they proceeded straightway, and

On the third day they reached the appointed field.

There the hunter and the ensnarer rested at their seat.

One day, two days, they lurked at the entrance to the well,

where the cattle were accustomed to slake their thirst,

where the creatures of the waters were sporting.

Then [came] Enkidu, whose home was the mountains,

who with gazelles ate herbs,

and with the cattle slaked his thirst,

and with the creatures of the waters rejoiced his heart.

And Shamhat, the enticer of men, beheld him * * *

"Behold, there he is" (the hunter exclaimed); "now disclose thy womb,

uncover thy nakedness, and let him enjoy thy favours.

Be not ashamed, but yield to his sensuous lust.

He shall see thee and shall approach unto thee;

Remove thy garment, and he shall lie in thine arms;

satisfy his desire after the manner of women;

then his cattle, raised with him on the field, shall forsake him

while he firmly presses his breast upon thine."

And Shamhat disclosed her womb, uncovered her nakedness, and let him enjoy her favours.

She was not ashamed, but yielded to his sensuous lust.

She removed her garment, he lay in her arms,

and she satisfied his desire after the manner of women.

He pressed his breast firmly upon hers.

For six days and seven nights Enkidu enjoyed the love of Shamhat.

And when he had sated himself with her charms,

he turned his countenance toward his cattle.

The gazelles, resting, beheld Enkidu; they and

the cattle of the field turned away from him.

This startled Enkidu and his body grew faint;

his knees became stiff, as his cattle departed,

and he became less agile than ever before.

And as he hearkened, he made a resolve.

He turned again, in love enthralled, to the feet of the harlot,

and gazed up into the face of the ensnarer.

And while the ensnarer spoke, his ears listened attentively;

and the siren spoke to Enkidu and said:

"Lofty thou art, Enkidu, thou shalt be like a god;Why, then, doest thou lie down with the beasts of the field?

Come, I will take thee to strong-walled Uruk;

to the glorious house, the dwelling of Anu and Ishtar,

the palace of Gilgamesh, (the hero) who is perfect in strength, surpassing, like a mountain bull, men in power."

While she spoke thus to him, he hearkened unto her

wise speech, and his heart yearned for a friend.

And Enkidu spoke unto her, the ensnarer:

"Come then, Shamhat, take me, and lead me

to the glorious dwelling, the sacred seat of Anu and Ishtar,

to the palace * of Gilgamesh, (the hero) who is perfect in

strength, surpassing, like as a mountain bull, men in power."

Here the text becomes very broken, only the latter half of a number of lines being preserved. As to the contents, this much may be said: Enkidu intends to test the strength of the famous hero (Gilgamesh)—whose friendship he desires—by means of a "lion, born in the desert and powerful in strength." New fragments found and skilfully placed together by Professor Haupt, have enabled Dr. Jeremias to partially restore the following narrative:

The Shamhat leads Enkidu to Uruk. As they arrived, the inhabitants of Uruk, clothed "in festive garments," were celebrating a festival—perhaps the Tammuz festival. The end of Col. V seems to be a warning to Enkidu, received in a dream:

"Gilgamesh will behold [thee].

I behold [* * *] his face,

it glows with heroic courage.

Strength he possesses, [magnificent?] is his whole body.

His power is stronger than thine.

He rests not [nor tires?], neither by day nor by night.

O Enkidu, change thy [intention?].

Shamash loves Gilgamesh;

Anu, Bel, and Ea are whispering (wisdom) into his ear.

Ere thou earnest down from the mountain

Gilgamesh beheld thee in a dream in Uruk."

Here the address seems to end, and the narrative returns to its hero, Gilgamesh, who also had a dream, and was troubled because he could not interpret it.

Gilgamesh came, to understand the dream, and said to his mother:

"My mother, I dreamed a dream in my nightly vision;

The stars of heaven, like Ami's host, fell upon me * * *"

The fragments of Col. VI contain another dream, the subject of which is likewise Enkidu and his adventures with the ensnarer Shamhat. The fragments indicate that the mother advised her son to make friendship with Enkidu, the giant. [i.e., wild man.]

[Here let us append the Pennsylvania tablet, covering the dream material and encounter with Shamhat found after the publication of this translation:]

Gilgamesh sought to interpret the dream;

Spoke to his mother:

"My mother, during my night

I became strong and moved about

among the heroes;

And from the starry heaven

A meteor(?) of Anu fell upon me:

I bore it and it grew heavy upon me,

I became weak and its weight I could not endure.

The land of Uruk gathered about it.

The heroes kissed its feet.

It was raised up before me.

They stood me up.

I bore it and carried it to thee."
The mother of Gilgamesh, who knows all things,
Spoke to Gilgamesh:
"Some one, O Gilgamesh, who like thee
In the field was born and
Whom the mountain has reared,
Thou wilt see (him) and [like a woman(?)] thou wilt rejoice.
Heroes will kiss his feet.
Thou wilt spare [him and wilt endeavor]
To lead him to me."
He slept and saw another
Dream, which he reported to his mother:
["My mother,] I have seen another
[Dream.] My likeness I have seen in the streets
[Of Uruk] of the plazas.
An axe was brandished, and
They gathered about him;
And the axe made him angry.
I saw him and I rejoiced,
I loved him as a woman,
I embraced him.
I took him and regarded him
As my brother."
The mother of Gilgamesh, who knows all things,
[Spoke to Gilgamesh]:
["O Gilgamesh, the man whom thou sawest,]
[Whom thou didst embrace like a woman].
(means) that he is to be associated with thee."
Gish understood the dream.

[As] Enki[du] was sitting before the woman,
[Her] loins(?) he embraced, her vagina(?) he opened.
[Enkidu] forgot the place where he was born.
Six days and seven nights
Enkidu continued
To cohabit with [the courtesan].
[The woman] opened her [mouth] and
Spoke to Enkidu:
"I gaze upon thee, O Enkidu, like a god art thou!
Why with the cattle
Dost thou [roam] across the field?
Come, let me lead thee
into [Uruk] of the plazas,
to the holy house, the dwelling of Anu,
O, Enkidu arise, let me conduct thee
To Eanna, the dwelling of Anu,
The place [where Gilgamesh is, perfect] in vitality.
And thou [like a wife wilt embrace] him.
Thou [wilt love him like] thyself.
Come, arise from the ground
(that is) cursed."
He heard her word and accepted her speech.
The counsel of the woman
Entered his heart.
She stripped off a garment,
Clothed him with one.
Another garment
She kept on herself.
She took hold of his hand.

Like [a god(?)] she brought him
To the fertile meadow,
The place of the sheepfolds.
In that place they received food;
[For he, Enkidu, whose birthplace was the mountain,]
[With the gazelles he was accustomed to eat herbs,]
[With the cattle to drink water,]
[With the water beings he was happy.]
(Perhaps one additional line missing.)
Milk of the cattle
He was accustomed to suck.
Food they placed before him,
He broke (it) off and looked
And gazed.
Enkidu had not known
To eat food.
To drink wine
He had not been taught.
The woman opened her mouth and
Spoke to Enkidu:
"Eat food, O Enkidu,
The provender of life!
Drink wine, the custom of the land!"
Enkidu ate food
Till he was satiated.
Wine he drank,
Seven goblets.
His spirit was loosened, he became hilarious.
His heart became glad and

His face shone.
[The barber(?)] removed
The hair on his body.
He was anointed with oil.
He became manlike.
He put on a garment,
He was like a man.
He took his weapon;
Lions he attacked,
(so that) the night shepherds could rest.
He plunged the dagger;
Lions he overcame.
The great [shepherds] lay down;
Enkidu was their protector.
The strong man,
The unique hero,
To [the shepherds(?)] he speaks:

(About thirteen lines missing.)

Making merry.
He lifted up his eyes,
He sees the man.
He spoke to the woman:
"O, courtesan, lure on the man.
Why has he come to me?
His name I will destroy."
The woman called to the man
Who approaches to him and he beholds him.

"Away! why dost thou [quake(?)]
Evil is the course of thy activity."
Then he opened his mouth and
Spoke to Enkidu:
"[To have (?)] a family home
Is the destiny of men, and
The prerogative(?) of the nobles.
For the city(?) load the workbaskets!
Food supply for the city lay to one side!
For the King of Uruk of the plazas,
Open the hymen(?), perform the marriage act!
For Gilgamesh, the King of Uruk of the plazas,
Open the hymen(?),
Perform the marriage act!
With the legitimate wife one should cohabit.
So before,
As well as in the future.
By the decree pronounced by a god,
From the cutting of his umbilical cord
(Such) is his fate."
At the speech of the hero
His face grew pale.

(About nine lines missing.)

[Enkidu] went [in front],
And the courtesan behind him.
He entered into Uruk of the plazas.
The people gathered about him.

As he stood in the streets
Of Uruk of the plazas,
The men gathered,
Saying in regard to him:
"Like the form of Gilgamesh he has suddenly become;
shorter in stature.
[In his structure high(?)], powerful,
.... overseeing(?)
In the land strong of power has he become.
Milk of cattle
He was accustomed to suck."
Steadily(?) in Uruk .....
The heroes rejoiced.
He became a leader.
To the hero of fine appearance,
To Gilgamesh, like a god,
He became a rival to him.
For Ishtar a couch
Was stretched, and
Gilgamesh [lay down, and afterwards(?)]
In the night he fled.
He approaches and
[Enkidu stood] in the streets.
He blocked the path
of Gilgamesh.
At the exhibit of his power,

(About seven lines missing.)

Strong(?) …

Gilgamesh

Against him [Enkidu proceeded],

[His hair] luxuriant.

He started [to go]

Towards him.

They met in the plaza of the district.

Enkidu blocked the gate

With his foot,

Not permitting Gilgamesh to enter.

They seized (each other), like oxen,

They fought.

The threshold they demolished;

The wall they impaired.

Gilgamesh and Enkidu

Seized (each other).

Like oxen they fought.

The threshold they demolished;

The wall they impaired.

Gilgamesh bent

His foot to the ground,

His wrath was appeased,

His breast was quieted.

When his breast was quieted,

Enkidu to him

Spoke, to Gilgamesh:

"As a unique one, thy mother

bore thee.

The wild cow of the stall,

Ninsun,

Has exalted thy head above men.

Kingship over men

Enlil has decreed for thee.

Second tablet,

enlarged beyond [the original(?)].

240 lines.

[End supplement.]

TABLET III

A great and important factor in the subsequent adventures of Gilgamesh is the fact that Enkidu becomes the friend and companion of the hero. Two fragments, published on pages 14 and 15 of Professor Haupt's edition, are supposed by Dr. Jeremias to have belonged to Cols. III and IV of this tablet. The former seems to be an address to a woman (the Shamhat?):

* * * the gods let thee enter

* * * forsaken was

* * * the consort * * *

* * * and he saw it alone,

and he relieved his heart and spoke to his friend.

* * * a dream I dreamed in my night's sleep,

[The stars?] of heaven fell upon the earth.

[Frightened?] I stood there.

* * * his face became disturbed

* * * like lion's claws were his nails

* * * the dream?] strengthened me * * *

The second fragment was a dialogue between Shamash, the sun god, and Enkidu, in consequence of which Enkidu's "angry heart became quieted." It seems that Shamash induced Enkidu, who is anxious to return to his mountain home, to remain. The Shamhat again plays a prominent role, and we hear of the promise to Enkidu of royal honours, the friendship and brotherly love of Gilgamesh. Says Shamash:

"Come, and on a fine, grand couch,

on a fine couch he [Gilgamesh] will let thee recline.

He will place thee upon a couch, a seat to the left.

The kings of the earth shall kiss thy feet.

The people of Uruk shall whine before thee * * *

and the nations shall work for thee.

* * * after thee shall be carried, whatever there be

* * * in the midst thereof he shall encamp."

Enkidu listened to the word of Shamash, the warrior hero,

* * * his angry heart became quieted.

A continuation of this tablet Dr. Jeremais believes to have found on page 87 of Haupt's edition. Here Gilgamesh promises to Enkidu precisely the same that Shamash promises on page 15 (see above). The gods have a purpose in view in bringing about friendship between Enkidu and Gilgamesh. The fragments of Tablets IV and V give us the key to it. They relate the battle of the city of Uruk against the Elamitic despot Humbaba, ending in the death of the latter and the enthronement of Gilgamesh as King of Uruk. The gods, being deeply interested in the destruction of Humbaba and the end of the rule of the hostile god [giant] Humba, take part in the fight. It is evident that this poetic narrative is simply the mythical representation of a great national upheaval, by means of which an Elamitic dynasty was overthrown and a Babylonian rule established.

TABLET IV

is represented by only a few small fragments, which, however, enable us to see that the tablet describes the preparation for the capture of the fortress of the Elamitic king, Humbaba. These two tablets (IV and V) then contain the historic kernel of the narrative of the epic. According to Dr. Jeremias, Tablet IV contained something like this: Col. I. Enkidu stands before the king of the gods (Marduk?), speaking probably of Humbaba, whom he and Gilgamesh intended to kill, and whose corpse vultures (?) may devour; they asked the god to be favourable to their fight.

We did look after thee, O king [of the gods?].

Now look thou also after us.

Gilgamesh then advises Enkidu to go

To the lofty palace of the great queen, who knoweth all.

Thereupon both go to the great prophetess, who is described in Col. II, her breast ornaments and her crown being especially mentioned. After this the narrative continues as follows:

[Before] Shamash he sacrificed a smoke-offering,

poured out a drink-offering;

lifted up before Shamash his hand,1 (praying):

"Why hast thou disquieted the heart of Gilgamesh?

Now thou hast taught him, and

a far road he travels unto Humbaba.

An unknown fight he is about to enter,

To an unknown war he is about to set forth.

From the day that he goeth, until he returneth again,

until he comes to the (splendid) cedar wood,

until he shall have killed Humbaba the despot,

all the many evils which shall befall him, shall ruin him.

On the day when thou * * *

The end of Col. II narrates the preparation for the great fight.

The forces of the country assembled together;

the army completed its preparations;

and the heroes put on their armour.

Then the two friends set out together. Col. V opens with these words:

In order that the cedar wood remain intact, Bel has made it a terror for the people.

The roaring of Humbaba was like that of a storm cyclone;

his mouth was (full of) blasphemy, his breath (killing?)

like hot wind;

* * * hears a roaring in the forest;

whosoever descends into his park.

In order that the cedar forest remain intact, Bel has

made it a terror for the people.

Whosoever enters it, pestilence (?) will overtake him.

And Gilgamesh spoke unto Enkidu, and said:

Plates 57 and 58 Dr. Jeremias assigns to the last column of Tablet IV. Gilgamesh recounts to Enkidu

a favourable dream,

a splendid dream,

in which he saw the corpse of Humbaba. Then they set out on their way in the morning;

every twenty double leagues they took a meal;

every thirty double leagues they took a rest.

Before Shamash they dug a hole.

Then Gilgamesh went up to * * *

and poured his sacrificial meal into the hole (saying):

"Mountain, bring a dream unto Enkidu!

Let him see dream-visions, O Shamash."

Then they go to sleep. About midnight Gilgamesh awakes, arises, and speaks to his friend Enkidu:

"My friend, hast thou called me?" Then he tells him of a

third dream that he had seen.

The dream that I dreamed was very terrible (?);

heaven thundered, earth quaked;

day grew dark, darkness came up;

lightning set in, fire flared up

sated [with destruction] and filled with death.

Then suddenly the light darkened, the fire was quenched

* * * fell down, turned into smoke * * *"

Enkidu heard this dream and said to him:

[The rest of this tablet is broken away.]

[Here let us append the Babylonian Yale tablet, which relates material about the preparations for battle with Humbaba.]

.... (my friend?)

[Something] that is exceedingly difficult,

[Why] dost thou desire

[to do this?]

.... something (?) that is very [difficult (?)],

[Why dost thou] desire

[to go down to the forest]?

A message [they carried] among [men]

They carried about.

They made a ....

.... they brought

(About 17 lines missing.)

.... my friend

.... they raised .....

answer [they returned.]

[To] the woman

They proceeded to the overthrowing

(About eleven lines missing.)

.... name(?) ....

[The one who is] a rival [to him]

subdue and ....

Wailing ....

The mother [of Gilgamesh, who knows everything]

Before [Shamash raised her hand]

Who

Now(?) [why]

hast thou stirred up the heart for my son,

[Restlessness imposed upon him (?)]

(About four lines missing.)

The eyes [of Enkidu filled with tears].
[He clutched] his heart;
[Sadly(?)] he sighed.
[The eyes of En]kidu filled with tears.
[He clutched] his heart;
[Sadly(?)] he sighed.
The face [of Gilgamesh was grieved].
[He spoke] to Enkidu:
["My friend, why are] thy eyes
[Filled with tears]?
Thy [heart clutched]
Dost thou sigh [sadly(?)]?"
[Enkidu opened his mouth] and
spoke to Gilgamesh:
"Attacks, my friend,
have exhausted my strength(?).
My arms are lame,
my strength has become weak."
Gilgamesh opened his mouth and
spoke to Enkidu:

(About four lines missing.)

..... [until] Ḫumbaba, [the terrible],
....
.... [I destroyed].

[I will go down to the] cedar forest,
.... the jungle
.... tambourine (?)
.... I will open it.
Enkidu opened his mouth and
spoke to Gilgamesh:
"Know, my friend, in the mountain,
when I moved about with the cattle
to a distance of one double hour into the heart of the forest,
[Alone?] I penetrated within it,
[To] Ḫumbaba, whose roar is a flood,
whose mouth is fire,
whose breath is death.
Why dost thou desire
To do this?
To advance towards
the dwelling(?) of Ḫumbaba?"
Gilgamesh opened his mouth and
[spoke to Enkidu:
"... [the covering(?)] I will destroy.
....[in the forest]
....
....
To ....
The dwelling [of Ḫumbaba]
The axe ....
Thou ....
I will [go down to the forest]."
Enkidu opened his mouth and

spoke to [Gilgamesh:]
"When [together(?)] we go down
To the [cedar] forest,
whose guardian, O warrior Gilgamesh,
a power(?) without [rest(?)],
Ḫumbaba, an offspring(?) of ....
Adad ....
He ....
To keep safe [the cedar forest],
[Enlil has decreed for it] seven-fold terror."
Gilgamesh [opened] his mouth and
spoke to [Enkidu]:
"Whoever, my friend, overcomes (?) [terror(?)],
it is well (for him) with Shamash for the length of [his days].
Mankind will speak of it at the gates.
Wherever terror is to be faced,
Thou, forsooth, art in fear of death.
Thy prowess lacks strength.
I will go before thee.
Though thy mouth calls to me; "thou art afraid to approach."
If I fall, I will establish my name.
Gilgamesh, the corpse(?) of Ḫumbaba, the terrible one,
has snatched (?) from the time that
My offspring was born in ......
The lion restrained (?) thee, all of which thou knowest.
....
.... thee and
.... open (?)
.... like a shepherd(?) .....

[When thou callest to me], thou afflictest my heart.
I am determined
[to enter] the cedar forest.
I will, indeed, establish my name.
[The work(?)], my friend, to the artisans I will entrust.
[Weapons(?)] let them mould before us."
[The work(?)] to the artisans they entrusted.
A dwelling(?) they assigned to the workmen.
Hatchets the masters moulded:
Axes of 3 talents each they moulded.
Lances the masters moulded;
Blades(?) of 2 talents each,
A spear of 30 mina each attached to them.
The hilt of the lances of 30 mina in gold
Gilgamesh and [Enki]du were equipped with 10 talents each
.... in Uruk seven its ....
.... the people heard and ....
[proclaimed(?)] in the street of Uruk of the plazas.
..... Gilgamesh [brought him out(?)]
[In the street (?)] of Uruk of the plazas
[Enkidu(?)] sat before him
..... [thus] he spoke:
"........ [of Uruk] of the plazas
.... [before him]
Gilgamesh of whom they speak, let me see!
whose name fills the lands.
I will lure him to the cedar forest,
Like a strong offspring of Uruk.
I will let the land hear (that)

I am determined to lure (him) in the cedar (forest).
A name I will establish."
The elders of Uruk of the plazas
brought word to Gilgamesh:
"Thou art young, O Gish, and thy heart carries thee away.
Thou dost not know what thou proposest to do.
We hear that Humbaba is enraged.
Who has ever opposed his weapon?
To one [double hour] in the heart of the forest,
Who has ever penetrated into it?
Ḫumbaba, whose roar is a deluge,
whose mouth is fire, whose breath is death.
Why dost thou desire to do this?
To advance towards the dwelling (?) of Ḫumbaba?"
Gilgamesh heard the report of his counsellors.
He saw and cried out to [his] friend:
"Now, my friend, thus [I speak].
I fear him, but [I will go to the cedar forest(?)];
I will go [with thee to the cedar forest].

(About five lines missing.)

May .... thee
Thy god may (?) .... thee;
On the road may he guide [thee in safety(?)].
At the rampart of [Uruk of the plazas],
Gilgamesh kneeled down [before Shamash(?)],
A word then he spoke [to him]:
"I will go, O Shamash, [thy] hands [I seize hold of].

When I shall have saved [my life],
Bring me back to the rampart [in Uruk].
Grant protection [to me ?]!"
Gilgamesh cried, "[my friend] ......
His oracle ....
....
....
....
When (?)

(About two lines missing.)

"[I(?)] Gilgamesh, the strong one (?) of the land.
...... A road which I have never [trodden];
.... food ...... do not (?) know.
[When] I shall have succeeded,
[I will praise] thee in the joy of my heart,
[I will extol (?)] the superiority of thy power,
[I will seat thee] on thrones."
.... his vessel(?)
The masters [brought the weapons (?)];
[bow] and quiver
They placed in hand.
[He took] the hatchet.
.... his quiver.
..... [to] the god(?) a second time
[With his lance(?)] in his girdle,
.... they took the road.
[Again] they approached Gilgamesh!

"How long] till thou returnest to Uruk?"
[Again the elders] approached him.
[For] the road they counselled Gilgamesh:
"Do [not] rely, O Gilgamesh, on thy strength!
Provide food and save thyself!
Let Enkidu go before thee.
He is acquainted with the way, he has trodden the road
[to] the entrance of the forest.
of Ḫumbaba all of them his ......
[He who goes] in advance will save the companion.
Provide for his [road] and [save thyself]!
(May) Shamash [carry out] thy endeavor!
May he make thy eyes see the prophecy of thy mouth.
May he track out (for thee) the closed path!
May he level the road for thy treading!
May he level the mountain for thy foot!
During thy night the word that wilt rejoice
may Lugal-banda convey, and stand by thee
in thy endeavor!
Like a youth may he establish thy endeavor!
In the river of Ḫumbaba as thou plannest,
wash thy feet!
Round about thee dig a well!
May there be pure water constantly for thy libation
Goblets of water pour out to Shamash!
[May] Lugal-banda take note of it!"
[Enkidu] opened his mouth and spoke to Gilgamesh:
"[Since thou art resolved] to take the road.
Thy heart [be not afraid,] trust to me!

[Confide] to my hand his dwelling(?)!"

[on the road to] Ḫumbaba they proceeded.

.... command their return

(Three lines missing.)

.... were filled.

.... they will go with me.

....

.... joyfully.

[Upon hearing] this word of his,

Alone, the road(?) [he levelled].

"Go, O Gilgamesh [I will go before thee(?)].

May thy god(?) go ....

May he show [thee the road !] .....

Gilgamesh and [Enkidu]

Knowingly ....

Between [them] ....

[End supplement]

TABLET V

Col. I. The heroes are in the sacred forest, surrounding the stronghold of Humbaba. They had apparently forced open its gate:

There they stood, lofty arose the forest, and

(astonished) they gazed at the height of the cedars

and at the entrance of the cedar wood,

where Humbaba was wont to walk with lofty steps.

Ways were laid out and paths well kept.

They saw the cedar hill, the dwelling of gods, the sanctuary

of Ernini. In front of the hill (mountain) a cedar stood of great

splendour, fine and good was its shade, filling with gladness (the heart?).

The remainder of the column is broken off, but it probably gave a further description of the palace and its surroundings.

Page 27 contains fragments of an address by Gilgamesh to Enkidu in which again is mentioned

The corpse to be devoured by the vultures.

In Cols. II and III (pp. 25 and 28, and perhaps also pp. 74 and 86) the heroes recount their former glorious deeds, a favourable indication for the success of their imminent battle with Humbaba. Of the other columns only a fragment of the closing lines of Col. V is preserved (p. 26), where, in the last line, the "head of Humbaba" is mentioned, a fact which proves that the preceding lines contained an account of the fight and slaying of Humbaba. Immediately upon this line follow, according to the custom of Babylonian scribes, two lines, one giving the first line of the next (VI) tablet, and the other stating that it was the V tablet of the whole series, the words of the first line of Tablet I being used as "catchword" for the whole epic. Both served as a guide for the reader of the whole series.

TABLET VI

narrates the celebration of the victory of Gilgamesh, and his repulse of Ishtar's love advances (Haupt, pp. 42-50).

He cleansed his weapons, he polished his arms.

He took off the armour that was upon him. He put away

his soiled garments and put on clean raiment;

clothed himself with his ornaments, put on his diadem (?).

Gilgamesh placed upon his head the crown and put on his diadem (?).

To win the favour and love of Gilgamesh, Ishtar, the lofty goddess desired (and said unto him):

"Come, Gilgamesh, be thou my spouse,

Give, O give unto me thy manly strength.

Be thou my husband, let me be thy wife, and I will set thee in a chariot (embossed) with precious stones and gold,

with wheels made of gold, and shafts of sapphires (?).

Large kudanu-lions thou shalt harness to it.

Under sweet-smelling cedars thou shalt enter into our house.

And] when thou enterest into our house

Thou shalt sit upon?] a lofty throne, and people shall kiss thy feet;

kings and lords and rulers shall bow down before thee.

Whatever mountain and country produces, they shall bring to thee as tribute.

* * *] thy sheep shall bear twin-ewes.

* * *] mules they shall bring as tribute.

Thy [majesty?] shall sit upon a chariot that is splendid,

drawn?] by a span that has no equal.

But Gilgamesh opened his mouth and spoke unto her; said unto the lofty goddess Ishtar:

The beginning lines of his speech are almost lost, only a few fragments being preserved. Gilgamesh refused the proffered love of Ishtar, reminding her that all her former lovers have come to grief through her, and said that he was not willing to share their fate.

"Where is thy husband Tammuz, who was to be forever?

What, indeed, has become of the allallu-bird * * *?

Well, I will tell thee plainly the dire result of thy coquetries.

To Tammuz, the husband of thy youth,
thou didst cause weeping and didst bring grief upon him every year.
The allallu-bird, so bright of colours, thou didst love;
But its wing thou didst break and crush,
so that now it sits in the woods crying: 'O my wing!'
Thou didst also love a lion, powerful in his strength,
seven and seven times didst thou dig a snaring pit for him.
Thou didst also love a horse, pre-eminent in battle,
but with bridle (?), spur, and whip thou didst force it on,
didst force it to run seven double-leagues at a stretch.
And when it was tired and wanted to drink, thou still didst force it on,
thereby causing weeping and grief to its mother Si-li-li.
Thou didst also love a shepherd of the flock * * *
who continually poured out incense before thee,
and, for thy pleasure, slaughtered lambs day by day.
Thou didst smite him, and turn him into a tiger,
so that his own sheep-boys drove him away,
and his own dogs tore him to pieces.
Thou didst also love a farmer, a gardener of thy father,
who continually brought unto thee dainties,
and daily adorned thy table for thee.
Thine eye thou didst cast on him and turn his mind, saying:
'Oh, my farmer boy, let us enjoy thy manly strength.
Let thy hand come forth and take away my virginity' (?).
But the farmer spoke unto thee and said:
'Me!—what is this that thou askest of me?
Mother, thou hast not baked, and I will not eat;
The food that I shall eat is bad and bitter,
and it is covered with cold and numbness.'

And when thou didst hear such words,
thou didst smite him and change him into a cripple(?)
And didst thus compel him to lie on a couch,
so that he could no more rise up from his bed.
And now thou wouldst also love me; but like unto them I would fare."
When Ishtar heard such words
she became enraged, and went up into heaven,
and came unto Anu [her father], and
To Antum (her mother) she went, and thus spoke (unto them):
"My father, Gilgamesh has insulted me;
Gilgamesh has upbraided me with my evil deeds,
my deeds of evil and of violence."
And Anu opened his mouth and spoke—
said unto her, the mighty goddess Ishtar:
"Thou shalt not remain so disconsolate,
even though Gilgamesh has upbraided thee with thy evil deeds,
thy deeds of evil and of violence."
And Ishtar opened her mouth and said,
she spoke unto Anu, her father:
"My father, create [for me] a heaven-bull."

The following seventy lines have come down in a very mutilated condition; and the meaning can only be surmised. As Dr. Jeremias has ingeniously pointed out, the lines remind us of the threat of Gilgamesh, spoken before the ocean palace (Tablet X, Col. I), and especially of the analogous conditions found in the account of the "Descent of Ishtar into the Netherworld," where the courageous goddess in her wrath forces entrance to the Netherworld. As she threatened there, so now here, in heaven, she would smash everything, if her will and wish is not granted. Anu, her father, though hesitating, is forced to accede and creates the heaven-bull. And now Ishtar breaks out in these words: "I will have revenge." The account of the fight of the two heroes, Gilgamesh and Enkidu, against the heaven-bull is almost completely lost. Lines 122 and 123 appear to say:

They?] hunted him and Enkidu [attacked?] the heaven-bull,

* * * and grasped him by his heavy tail.

On an old Babylonian cylinder representing the fight we see the bull standing on its hind feet, Enkidu holding the monster by its head and tail, while Gilgamesh plunges the dagger into its heart. We can also gather from the remains of the lines that three hundred heroes took part in the fight. After the heroes had killed the bull and had thus satisfied their hearts, they brought unto Shamash, the sun god, a thank offering. The narrative then continues:

Then Ishtar went up to the wall of Uruk, the strong-walled;

she uttered a piercing cry and broke out into a curse, (saying):

"Woe to Gilgamesh, who thus has grieved me,

and has killed the heaven-bull."

But Enkidu, hearing these words of Ishtar,

tore out the right side of the heaven-bull,

and threw it into her face, (saying):

"And thus I will, indeed, defeat thee;

and I will do unto thee even as I have done to him;

I will hang its heart(?) upon thy side, forsooth."

Then Ishtar gathered her followers, that ruin men,

the hierodules and the sacred prostitutes.

Over the right side of the heaven-bull she wept and lamented.

But Gilgamesh assembled the people, and all his workmen.

The workmen admired the size of its horns.

Thirty minas of precious stones was their value;

half of an inch (?) in size was their thickness (?).

Six measures of oil they both could hold.

For the anointing of his god Lugal-tur-da8 he dedicated it.

He brought the horns and hung them up in the shrine of his lordship.

Then they washed their hands in the river Euphrates,

took the road, and set out (for the city),

and rode through the streets of the city of Uruk.

The people of Uruk assembled and looked with astonishment [at the heroes?].

Gilgamesh then spoke to the servants (?) of [his palace?]

and cried out unto them, (saying):

"Who is glorious among the heroes?

Who shines among the men?"

"Gilgamesh?] is glorious among the heroes,

Gilgamesh?] shines among the men!"

[Lines 204 to 206 are lost.]

and Gilgamesh held a joyful feast in his palace.

Then the heroes slept, stretched out upon their couches.

And Enkidu slept, and saw a vision in his sleep.

He arose (in the morning) and "solved" the dream,

and spoke unto Gilgamesh thus:

"My friend, wherefor have the great gods thus taken counsel?"

The last line of the sixth tablet represents, no doubt, the beginning of the next (the seventh) tablet. This line is followed as usual by the colophon, thus:

The sixth tablet of: "He who has seen the history of Gilgamesh."

TABLETS VII and VIII

Only a few fragments have been preserved, and very scanty information can be gathered from them. Tablet VII must have begun with Enkidu's account of his dream on the morning after the victory-jubilee in Uruk, and closed with the death of that hero, brought about by the goddess Ishtar. Pages 53 and 54 (cf. 55) of Professor Haupt's edition are said, by Dr. Jeremias, to belong to Tablet VIII, because the preceding column (a Column VI), being the obverse of the same tablet, speaks of the sickness and death of Enkidu (see Tablet IX). In Col. I, Enkidu calls on his friend to perform some heroic deed, worthy of his renown. They are halting in front of a forest gate, which Enkidu thus addresses:

There is none other tree like unto thee;

Six gar [1 gar = 12 or 14 cubits] *is* thy height and two gar thy thickness.

Enkidu also says of it, "I know thee." And in Col. VI he moans:

"In good health I went forth, my friend. * * *

But the dream which I dreamed has been fulfilled."

And there lay Enkidu for twelve days [on the first and the second day?]

on which Enkidu on his couch [lay sick?];

On the third and the fourth * * *;

On the fifth, sixth, seventh, eighth, etc., day

on which Enkidu [lay sick on his couch?]

The eleventh, the twelfth day * * *

On which Enkidu lay on his couch * * *

Then he called to Gilgamesh.

The few traces of the following lines still show that the hero received his wound in a fight which in fearful premonition "he had feared." The lament for the dead in Tablet XII shows that it must have been a very severe and unusual fight. Of his end, narrated, no doubt, on Tablet IX, it is said repeatedly in Tablet XII: "Earth has snatched him away."

TABLET IX

begins with the lament of Gilgamesh for the death of his friend, and with his resolve to go to his ancestor Utnapishtim, that he may learn the mystery of the latter's apotheosis, and, at the same time, secure recovery from a loathsome disease, with which Ishtar has smitten him.

Gilgamesh wept bitterly over the loss of his friend

Enkidu, and he lay stretched out upon the ground, (saying):

"I will not die like Enkidu,

But weeping has entered into my heart;

Fear of death has befallen me, and

I lie here stretched out upon the ground.

To (test) the strength of Utnapishtim, the son of Kidin- Marduk,

I will set out, and I will go at once."

"At the mountain ravine I arrived by night-time,

* * * Lions I saw, and I was afraid;

* * * but I lifted my head to god Sin and I prayed.

To the [great?] majesty of the god came my cry,

[and he hearkened] and saved me, even me."

And in the night he saw?] a vision and a dream,

Lions * * *] were enjoying themselves."

And he lifted the axe in his hand,

and drew out the sword from his belt.

Like a javelin he threw himself between them;

he wounded, killed, and scattered [them?]

[The rest of the column is lost.]

Col. II narrates the meeting of Gilgamesh with the scorpion-men, at the foot

of a mountain whose name is Mashu.

As he came to the mountain of Mashu,

whose entrance is guarded daily by monsters,

whose back extends to the dam of heaven,

and whose breast reaches down to Aralu,

Scorpion-men guard its gate;

Dreadful terror they spread, and it is death to behold them.

Their splendour is fearful, overthrowing the mountains;

From sunrise to sunset they guard the sun.

Gilgamesh beheld them, and with fear

and terror his face grew dark.

His mind became confused at the wildness of their aspect.

But one scorpion-man said to his wife:

"He that there cometh to us, flesh of the gods is his body."

And the wife answered the scorpion-man:

"Two (thirds) he resembles a god, and one third only a man."

And the scorpion-man replied and said unto her:

["One] of the gods has given the order;

[and] he has travelled over far-distant roads,

until he should come unto me.

The mountains] which he has crossed are steep."

[The remainder is broken away.]

Col. III, as far as the fragments permit us to see, narrates that Gilgamesh, seeing that the monster regarded him with friendly eyes, recovered from his fright and told the scorpion-man of his intention to go "to Utnapishtim, his ancestor, who had been removed into the assembly of the gods and [had thus power over] life and death." The scorpion-man replied by describing to Gilgamesh the difficulties and dangers connected with such a march through the mountain of Mashu. Nobody has yet been able to do so, twelve miles of heavy darkness in all directions having to be penetrated. But the hero was not discouraged, and the scorpion-man acceded to his urgent request and opened to him the gate of the mountain; and now begins the wearisome march:

One mile he marches, thick is the darkness, not does it grow light.

Two miles he marches, thick is the darkness, not does it grow light.

Col. V (p. 65) continues the description of the twelve-mile walk in the same diffuse epic style; then the hero leaves the mountain and—on the shore of the sea—beholds a beautiful and wonderful tree:

And as he saw it, he ran toward it.

Diamonds (?) it bore as fruit,

Branches were hanging (down?), beautiful to behold.

Crystal (antimony?) the branches bore;

with fruit it was laden, dazzling the eye (of the hero).

Other precious trees are also there.

In Col. VI Gilgamesh must have reached the seacoast, for

TABLET X

commences, as shown in the colophon to Tablet IX:

The (divine) girl Siduri, sitting upon the throne of the sea,

probably a poetic expression for the ocean-palace, in which she resides, as we are told later. In Col. II, Gilgamesh finds another obstacle in his way, as he arrived "clothed with a skin." Again, he began to lament and was angered at the " distant roads " that he had yet to travel.

Sirudi sees him from afar off,

and she speaks to herself

and [takes counsel] with herself:

"Because this * * *

How shall he succeed (?) in [his endeavour?]

And as Sirudi sees him approach she closes [her ocean-

palace?]

Its gate she closes and closes * * *

But Gilgamesh listens to * * *

Lifts up his finger (?) and * * *

Then Gilgamesh spoke unto Sirudi and said:

"Sirudi, what doest thou gaze [at me?].

Why doest thou bolt the gate against me?];

For I will break [thy gate"

The lower part of the plate is destroyed, and we can only conjecture that Sirudi described to the hero the impossibility of continuing his journey, which would lead him across an impassable sea. In Col. II the hero again tells the reason for his journey, and laments the loss of his beloved friend, Enkidu, who has now returned to dust, and to share whose lot seems unbearable to him.

And Gilgamesh said unto her, the Sirudi:

Tell me, O Sirudi, which is the way to Utnapishtim?

What is its direction, O Sirudi, tell me its direction.

If it be possible, I will cross the sea;

But if it is impossible, I will run there across the field."
And Sirudi answered unto Gilgamesh, and said:
"Gilgamesh, there has never been a crossing (here),
and no one since eternal days has ever crossed the sea.
Shamash, the hero, crosses it; but besides Shamash who
can cross it? Difficult is the crossing, and extremely dangerous the way,
and closed are the Waters of Death,which bolt its entrance.
How, then, Gilgamesh, wilt thou cross the sea?
And if thou should'st reach the Waters of Death, what wouldst thou do?
But Gilgamesh, there is Urshinabi, the sailor of Utnapishtim
at the side of those with stones'; in the forest he fells a cedar.
Him may thy countenance behold.
If possible, cross over with him; but if impossible, go back."
When Gilgamesh heard this,
he lifted up the axe at his arm,
drew the sword from his belt, slipped in and descended to [***];
and fell like a javelin between them.

The hero stands at the entrance to the Waters of Death, which are supposed to surround the ocean. The "Isle of the Blessed" is thought to be beyond these Waters of Death, just as in the case of the Netherworld. In Col. III Gilgamesh tells Urshinabi of his grief, using undoubtedly the same words as before, and closes with the request to ferry him over.

Urshinabi said unto Gilgamesh:

"Thy hand, O Gilgamesh, has prevented [the crossing].
Thou hast smashed 'those with stones' * * *
'Those with stones ' are now smashed and the * * * is no more.
Take, Gilgamesh, the axe at thy side,

go into the wood and make one hundred and twenty oars [punting-poles] five gar long."

He is also to make other preparations for his journey.

And Gilgamesh on hearing this (i. e., Urshinabi's instructions),

took the axe at his side, and [drew the sword from his belt].

He went into the woods and felled trees for one hundred and twenty oars five gar in length,

smeared them over with pitch and brought them [to Urshinabi].

Then Gilgamesh and Urshinabi embarked;

the ship tossed to and fro while they were on their way.

A journey of forty and five days they accomplished within three days,

and thus Urshinabi arrived at the Waters of Death.

And now they begin to face the most serious dangers. Col. IV relates that the ferryman advises the hero not to give in, as long as the journey upon the Waters of Death lasts. Many a day they spent on their journey, and day after day Gilgamesh stuck to the oar;

and then Gilgamesh loosened his belt (i. e., rested from his exertions),

for he was weary.

And Utnapishtim looking at him from the distance

Began thinking within himself, and

With himself he thus meditated:

"Why are ['those with stones'] of the ship smashed?

And one, who has not my * * * rides in [the ship].

He that comes there [is he?] not a man, and has he not

the 'right side' of a man?

I look: (Is that) * * * not [a human being?]

I look: (Is that) * * * not [a man?]

I look: (Is that) * * * [not a god?]

He resembles me in every respect."

At the beginning of Col. V, Gilgamesh drew nigh unto the shore safely and, while still sitting in the ship, he poured out his tale of woe before his ancestor; he told him of the adventures which he and his friend had encountered, among which was one with a " panther of the field "; then follows an account of the killing of the heaven-bull; the slaying of Humbaba, the despot, who had lived in a cedar forest; other adventures with tigers; his friend's sickness and sad death; and "now I weep because of him"; then he tells how he had wandered across all the countries, passed over steep mountains, and crossed dreadful seas, but all in vain:

"The friend whom I loved has been turned to clay; Enkidu, my friend.

And I will not, like unto him, lie down; not will I sink to where my friend is now."

And Gilgamesh said unto Utnapishtim:

"Here I have come, and Utnapishtim, whom people call the 'distant,' I will see.

To him I will turn (for help?); I have travelled through all the lands,

I have crossed over the steep mountains, and I have traversed all the seas," etc.

Col. VI must have contained a lengthy reply of Utnapishtim, telling him that he could do nothing to help him to escape from death. He told him that death comes to all, that none could escape from it.

As long as houses are built, as long as tablets are sealed,

as long as brothers are at enmity,

as long as there exist strife and hatred in the land,

as long as the river carries the waters (to the sea?), etc.,

so long is there no likeness of death drawn (i. e., no man can tell when his own time might come).

When the alu-demon and the eziz-demon greetaman,

then the Anunnaki, the great gods [assemble]

and the goddess of fate, she who with them determines fate, will do so,

For they determine death and life.

But the days of death are unknown to mankind.

Then follows the colophon stating that this was the tenth tablet of the great epic.

TABLET XI

contains the famous account of the deluge. The text of this tablet is published by Friedrich Delitzsch in his "Assyrische Lesestticke," third edition, pp. 101-109; *and*more recently, by Professor Haupt in the second part of his "Das Babylonische Nimrodepos," pp. 133-150, this latter being a complete, critical text, giving all the variant readings and additional remarks beneath the text.1 The original publication on plates 50 and 51 in the fourth volume of the "Inscriptions of Western Asia" has been re-edited, with many improvements, in the second edition of this volume, by Theophilus G. Pinches, in 1891 (plates 43 and 44).—Translations of the deluge story (lines 1-104 of Haupt's edition), or of parts thereof, have been made, since the days of George Smith, by many Assyriologists—e. g., Fox Talbot, Jules Oppert, F. Lenormant. Special attention is called here to the following translations: I. Peter Jensen, in his " Cosmology of the Babylonians" (pp. 365446), and in "Assyrisch-babylonische Mythen und Epen," pp. 228-257; 2. Alfred Jeremias, in his " Izdubar-Nimrod" (pp. 32-40, translating the whole eleventh tablet); 3. H. Winckler, " Keilinschriftliches Textbuch zum Alten Testament " (pp. 70-87); 4. Heinrich Zimmern in Gnnkel's book on " Creation and Chaos" (pp. 423-428); 5. L. W. King, "First Steps in Assyrian" (London, 1898, pp. 161-181, text, transliteration, and translation), and the same author's "Babylonian Religion and Mythology" (London, 1899, chap, iv, pp. 121-146); 6. C. J. Ball, "Light from the East, or the Witness of the Monuments" (London, 1899, pp. 34 foll.); 7. According to Professor Jastrow's statement on p. 730 of his "Religion of Babylonia and Assyria," the transliteration and translation of the deluge text, together with critical notes and commentary, by Professor Haupt in the forthcoming third edition of Schrader's "Die Keilinschriften und das Alte Testament," is to be by far the best ever published.—In general, see also the article "Deluge," by H. Zimmern and T. K. Cheyne in Cheyne and Black's

"Encyclopaedia Biblica," London, 1899, vol. i, cols. 1055-1066.

Tablet XI continues the dialogue between Utnapishtim and Gilgamesh, begun in Cols. V and VI of the preceding tablet.

Gilgamesh said to him, to Utnapishtim, the distant:"I gazeupon thee (in amazement), O Utnapishtim!

Thy appearance has not changed, like unto me thou art also.

And thy nature itself has not changed, like unto me thou art also,

though thou hast departed this life. But my heart has still to struggle

against all that no longer (?) lies upon thee.

Tell me, How didst thou come to dwell (here?) and obtain eternal life among the gods?"

[From the shore Utnapishtim, the favourite of the gods, now relates the story of the deluge to the hero, who, sitting in his ship, is listening to him.]

Utnapishtim then said unto Gilgamesh:

"I will reveal unto thee, O Gilgamesh, the mysterious story,

and the mystery of the gods I will tell thee.

The city of Shurippak, a city which, as thou knowest,

is situated on the bank of the river Euphrates.

That city was corrupt, so that the gods within it

decided to bring about a deluge, even the great gods,

as many as?] there were: their father, Anu;

their counsellor, the warrior Bel;

their leader, Ninib;

their champion, the god En-nu-gi.

But Ea, the lord of unfathomable wisdom, argued with them.

Their plan he told to a reed-hut, (saying):

'Reed-hut, reed-hut, clay-structure, clay-structure!
Reed-hut, hear; clay-structure, pay attention!
Thou man of Shurippak, son of Ubara-Tutu,
Build a house, construct a ship;
Forsake thy possessions, take heed for thy life!
Abandon thy goods, save (thy) life,
and bring living seed of every kind into the ship.
As for the ship, which thou shalt build,
let its proportions be well measured:
Its breadth and its length shall bear proportion each to each,
and into the sea then launch it.'
I took heed, and said to Ea, my lord:
'I will do, my lord, as thou hast commanded;
I will observe and will fulfil the command.
But what shall I answer to (the inquiries of) the city,
the people, and the elders?'
Ea opened his mouth and spoke,
and he said unto me, his servant:
'Man, as an answer say thus unto them:
"I know that Bel hates me. No longer can I live in your city;
Nor on Bel's territory can I live securely any longer; I will go down to the 'deep,' I will live with Ea, my lord.
Upon you he will (for a time?) pour down rich blessing.
He will grant you] fowl [in plenty] and fish in abundance,
Herds of cattle and an abundant] harvest.
Shamash has appointed a time when the rulers of darkness
at eventide will pour down upon you] a destructive rain."'

The lower part of Col. I is unfortunately much mutilated. Line 48 seems to read:

As soon as early dawn appeared.

Then continues line 55:

The brightness [of day?] I feared;
All that was necessary I collected together.
On the fifth day I drew its design;
In its middle part its sides were ten gar high;
Ten gar also was the extent of its deck;
I added a front-roof to it and closed it in.
I built it in six stories,
thus making seven floors in all;
The interior of each I divided again into nine partitions.
Beaks for water within I cut out.
I selected a pole and added all that was necessary.
Three (variant, five) šhar of pitch I smeared on its outside;
three shar of asphalt I used for the inside (so as to make
it water-tight).
Three shar of oil the men carried, carrying it in vessels.
One shar of oil I kept out and used it for sacrifices,
while the other two shar the boatman stowed away.
For the temple of the gods (?) I slaughtered oxen;
I killed lambs (?) day by day.
Jugs of cider (?), of oil, and of sweet wine,
Large bowls (filled therewith?), like river water (i. e., freely)
I poured out as libations.
I made a feast (to the gods) like that of the New-Year's Day.
To god Shamash my hands brought oil.

[* * *] the ship was completed.

[* * *] heavy was the work, and

I added tackling above and below, [and after all was finished] ,

The ship sank into water] two thirds of its height.

With all that I possessed I filled it;

with all the silver I had I filled it;

with all the gold I had I filled it;

with living creatures of every kind I filled it.

Then I embarked also all my family and my relatives,

cattle of the field, beasts of the field, and the uprighteous people—all them I embarked.

A time had Shamash appointed, (namely):

'When the rulers of darkness send at eventide a destructive rain,

then enter into the ship and shut its door.'

This very sign came to pass, and

The rulers of darkness sent a destructive rain at eventide.

I saw the approach of the storm,

and I was afraid to witness the storm;

I entered the ship and shut the door.

I intrusted the guidance of the ship to Purur-bel, the boatman,

the great house, and the contents thereof.

As soon as early dawn appeared,

there rose up from the horizon a black cloud,

within which the weather god (Adad) thundered,

and Nabu and the king of the gods (Marduk) went before.

The destroyers passed across mountain and dale (literally, country).

Dibbara, the great, tore loose the anchor-cable (?).

There went Ninib and he caused the banks to overflow;

the Anunnaki lifted on high (their) torches,

and with the brightness thereof they illuminated the universe.

The storm brought on by Adad swept even up to the heavens

and all light was turned into darkness.

[ ] overflooded the land like * * *

It blew with violence and in one day (?) it rose above the mountains (??).

Like an onslaught in battle it rushed in on the people.

Not could brother look after brother.

Not were recognised the people from heaven.

The gods even were afraid of the storm;

they retreated and took refuge in the heaven of Anu.

There the gods crouched down like dogs, on the inclosure of heaven they sat cowering.

Then Ishtar cried out like a woman in travail

and the lady of the gods lamented with a loud voice, (saying):

'The world of old has been turned back into clay,

because I assented to this evil in the assembly of the gods.

Alas! that when I assented to this evil in the council of the gods,

I was for the destruction of my own people.

What I have created, where is it?

Like the spawn of fish it fills the sea.'

The gods wailed with her over the Anunnaki.

The gods were bowed down, and sat there weeping.

Their lips were pressed together (in fear and in terror).

Six days and nights

The wind blew, and storm and tempest overwhelmed the country.

When the seventh day drew nigh the tempest, the storm, the battle

which they had waged like a great host began to moderate.

The sea quieted down; hurricane and storm ceased.

I looked out upon the sea and raised loud my voice,

But all mankind had turned back into clay.

Like the surrounding field had become the bed of the rivers.

I opened the air-hole and light fell upon my cheek.

Dumfounded I sank backward, and sat weeping, while over my cheek flowed the tears.

I looked in every direction, and behold, all was sea.

Now, after twelve (days?) there rose (out of the water) a strip of land.

To Mount Nisir the ship drifted.

On Mount Nisir the boat stuck fast and it did not slip away.

The first day, the second day, Mount Nisir held the ship fast, and did not let it slip away.

The third day, the fourth day, Mount Nisir held the ship fast, and did not let it slip away.

The fifth day, the sixth day, Mount Nisir held the ship,fast, and did not let it slip away.

When the seventh day drew nigh

I sent out a dove, and let her go.

The dove flew hither and thither,

but as there was no resting-place for her, she returned.

Then I sent out a swallow, and let her go.

The swallow flew hither and thither,

but as there was no resting-place for her she also returned.

Then I sent out a raven, and let her go.

The raven flew away and saw the abatement of the waters.

She settled down to feed, went away, and returned no more.

Then I let everything go out unto the four winds, and I offered a sacrifice.

I poured out a libation upon the peak of the mountain.

I placed the censers seven and seven,

and poured into them calamus, cedar-wood, and sweet incense.

The gods smelt the savour;

yea, the gods smelt the sweet savour;

the gods gathered like flies around the sacrificer.

But when now the lady of the gods (Ishtar) drew nigh,

she lifted up the precious ornaments (?)which Anu had made according to her wish (and said):

'Ye gods here! by my necklace, not will I forget.

These days will I remember, never will I forget (them).

Let the gods come to the offering;

But Bel shall not come to the offering,

Since rashly he caused the flood-storm,

and handed over my people unto destruction.'

Now, when Bel drew nigh,

and saw the ship, the god was wroth,

and anger against the gods, the Igigi, filled his heart, (and he said):

'Who then has escaped here (with his life)?

No man was to survive the universal destruction.'

Then Ninib opened his mouth and spoke,

saying unto Bel, the warrior:

'Who but Ea could have planned this!

For does not Ea know all arts?'

Then Ea opened his mouth and spoke,

saying unto Bel, the warrior:

'Ay, thou wise one among the gods, thou warrior,

how rash of thee to bring about a flood-storm!

On the sinner visit his sin,and on the wicked his wickedness;

but be merciful, forbear, let not all be destroyed!

Be considerate, let not everything be [confounded]!

Instead of sending a flood-storm,

let lions come and diminish mankind;

Instead of sending a flood-storm,
let tigers come and diminish mankind;
Instead of sending a flood-storm,
let famine come and smite the land;
Instead of sending a flood-storm,
let pestilence come and kill off the people.
I did not reveal the mystery of the great gods.
(Some one?) caused Atrachasis to see (it) in a dream, and so he (Utnapishtim) heard the mystery of the gods."
Thereupon Bel arrived at a decision.
Bel went up into the ship, took me by the hand and led me out.
He led out also my wife and made her kneel beside me;
He turned us face to face, and standing between us, blessed us, (saying)
'Ere this Utnapishtim was only human;
But now Utnapishtim and his wife shall be lofty like unto the gods;
Let Utnapishtim live far away (from men) at the mouth of the (two?) rivers.'
Then they took me and let us dwell far away at the mouth of the rivers."

After Utnapishtim had finished this account, he turned to Gilgamesh and said:

"Now as for thee, which one of the gods shall give thee strength,
that the life thou desirest thou shalt obtain?
Now sleep!" And for six days and seven nights
Gilgamesh resembled one lying lame.
Sleep came over him like a storm wind.
Then Utnapishtim said to his wife:
"Behold, here is the hero whose desire is life (= recovery)!
Sleep came upon him like a storm wind."
And the wife replied to Utnapishtim, the distant:

"Transform him; let the man eat of the charm-root.

Let him, restored in health, return on the road on which he came.

Let him pass out through the great door unto his own country."

And Utnapishtim said to his wife:

"The suffering (and torture) of the man pain thee.

Well, then, cook now for him the food and place it at his head."

And while Gilgamesh slept on board of his ship,

she cooked the food to place it at his head.

And while he slept on board of his ship,

firstly, his food was prepared (?);

secondly, it was peeled;

thirdly, it was moistened;

fourthly, his food (?) was cleaned;

fifthly, shiba (i. e., old age) was added;

sixthly, it was cooked;

seventhly, of a sudden the man was transformed, having eaten of the magic food.

Then spoke Gilgamesh, and said unto Utnapishtim, the distant:

"I had sunk down, and sleep had befallen me.

Of a sudden thou didst charm me, and thus help me" (?).

And Utnapishtim said unto Gilgamesh:

"* * * Gilgamesh partake of (?) thy food.

* * * shall be told unto thee:

firstly, thy food was prepared (?);

secondly, it was peeled;

thirdly, it was moistened;

fourthly, thy food (?) was cleaned;

fifthly, shipa was added;

sixthly, it was cooked;

seventhly, I transformed thee suddenly,
and thou didst eat of the magic food."
And Gilgamesh said unto Utnapishtim, the distant:
"What?] shall I do, Utnapishtim? whither shall I go?
The demon (of the dead?) has seized my [friend?].
Upon my couch death now sits.
And where my * * * there is death."
And Utnapishtim said to Urshabani, the ferryman:
"Urshabani, thou * * * at thy side (?), let the boat carry thee;
whosoever attempts to board [the ship?] exclude him from it.
The man, before whom thou goest,
has his body covered with sores,
and the eruption of his skin has altered the beauty of his body.
Take him, Urshabani, and bring him to the place of purification,
where he can wash his sores in water that they may become white as snow;
Let him cast off his (sore?) skin and the sea will carry it away;
His body shall then appear well (and healthy);
Let the turban also be replaced on his head,
and the garment that covers his nakedness.
Until he returns to his city,
until he arrives at his road.
The garment shall not shed [hair?], it shall remain entirely new."
And Urshabani took him and brought him to the place of purification,
where he washed his sores in water so that they became white as snow;
he cast off his (sore?) skin and the sea carried it away;
his body appeared well (and healthy) again;
He replaced also the turban on his head;
and the garment that covered his nakedness;
until he should return to his city;

until he should arrive at his road;

[the garment did not shed hair], it remained entirely new.

Then Gilgamesh and Urshabani embarked again,

and during their journey the ship tossed to and fro.

[After Gilgamesh and Urshabani had returned from the place of purification:]

The wife of Utnapishtim spoke unto her husband, the distant, (saying):

"Gilgamesh did go away, laboured, and has pulled (the oar?).

What now wilt thou do (or give), that he may return to his country?"

And Gilgamesh lifted up the pole, and drew the boat nearer to the shore.

Then Utnapishtim spoke unto Gilgamesh (and said):

"Gilgamesh, thou didst go away, didst labour and pull (the oar?).

What now shall I give thee, that thou mayest return to thy country?

I will reveal unto thee, Gilgamesh, a mystery,

and [the decision of the gods] I will announce unto thee.

There is a plant resembling buckthorn, its thorn (?) stings like that of a bramble.

When thy hands can reach that plant * * *

[The following lines 286-293 are greatly mutilated]

When Gilgamesh had heard this he opened the * * *

bound heavy stones [to his feet],

which dragged him down to the sea [and thus he found the plant].

Then he grasped the (magic) plant.

He removed [from his feet] the heavy stones [and one fell down?],

and a second he threw down to the [first?].

And Gilgamesh said unto Urshabani, the ferryman:

"Urshabani, this plant is a plant of great renown (or transformation?);

and what man desires in his heart, he obtains.

I will take it to Uruk the strong-walled, I will nurse (plant?) it there and then cut it off.

Its name is (?): 'Even an old man will be rejuvenated!'

I will eat of this and return (again) to the vigour of my youth."

[And now they start out to return home to Uruk the strong-walled.]

Every twenty double-leagues they then took a meal:

and every thirty double-leagues they took a rest.

And Gilgamesh saw a well wherein was cool (and refreshing) water;

He stepped into it and poured out some water.

A (demon in the shape of a) serpent darted out; the plant slipped [away from his hands];

he came [out of the well?], and took the plant away,

and as he turned back, he uttered a curse (?).

And after this Gilgamesh sat down and wept.

Tears flowed down his cheeks,

and he said unto Urshabani, the ferryman:

"Why, Urshabani, did my hands tremble?

Why did the blood of my heart stand still?

Not on myself did I bestow any benefit.

On the ground-lion (?) this benefit has been bestowed.

After a journey of only twenty double-leagues the plant has been snatched away,

As I opened the well, and lowered the vessel (?).

I see the sign, that has become an omen to me. I am to return,

leaving the ship on the shore."

Then they continued to take a meal every twenty double-leagues,

and every thirty double-leagues they took a rest,

until they arrived at Uruk the strong-walled.

Gilgamesh then spoke to Urshabani, the ferryman, (and said):

"Urshabani, ascend and walk about on the wall of Uruk,

Inspect the corner-stone, and examine its brick-work,

whether its wall is not made of burned brick, and its foundation (overlaid with?) pitch.

'Sevenfold is thy name' (?).

[The closing lines can not be correctly translated.]

Then follows the first line of Tablet XII; and the usual colophon indicating that the tablet is the eleventh of the Gilgamesh epic, copied faithfully from the original, and the property of Ashurbanipal.

TABLET XII

Only the second half of Col. I is preserved, and relates how Gilgamesh, after his return from this long journey, continued to lament over the loss of his friend Enkidu. Addressing him, though absent, he said:

"To a temple [thou goest no more?]

white garments [thou puttest on no more].

Like an ordinary mortal (?) thou art fallen.

With sweet-smelling bull's fat dost thou no more anoint thyself,

and people no more gather around thee on account of this sweet odour.

The bow no longer dost thou stretch upon the ground;

and those that were slain with the bow now are round about thee.

The staff no longer dost thou carry in thy hand;

The spirits of death have taken thee captive.

Sandals no longer dost thou tie to thy feet;

A (war) cry no longer dost thou shout here on earth;

Thy wife whom thou lovedst, no longer dost thou kiss;

Thy wife whom thou hatedst, no longer dost thou smite.

Thy son whom thou lovedst, no longer dost thou kiss;

Thy son whom thou hatedst, no longer dost thou smite.

The woes of the netherworld have overtaken thee; as well as

she that is dark, she that is dark, mother Nin-azu, who is dark,

whose white, shining body is not clothed with a garment,

whose breast like the bowl (lid?) of a case [is not * * *]." [Note: refers to Ereshkigal]

In Cols. II and III Gilgamesh goes alone into the temple of the god Ningul, and laments over the loss of his friend in similar words:

"His wife whom he loved, no longer does he kiss;

His wife whom he hated, no longer does he smite;

His son whom he loved, no longer does he kiss;

His son whom he hated, no longer does he smite.

The woes of earth have snatched him away, and

she that is dark, she that is dark, mother Nin-azu, who is dark,

whose white, shining body is not clothed with a garment,

whose breast like the bowl (lid?) of a box [is not * * *].

Enkidu has [gone down?] from earth into [darkness?]

pestilence has not snatched him away, consumption has not snatched him away;

earth has snatched him away.

The lurking demon of Nergal, the merciless, has not snatched him away,

earth has snatched him away.

The battlefield has not slain him; earth has snatched him away."

[While Gilgamesh spoke thus?] Ningul wept for his servant Enkidu.

Then Gilgamesh went alone to E-kur the Temple of Bel (Marduk?) (and prayed):

"Father Bel, the sting of a fly has cast me down upon the ground;

Insects have brought me low to the ground.

Enkidu [has sunk down] to the shades;

Pestilence has not snatched him away, etc. * * *

The lurking demon of Nergal, the merciless [has not snatched him away].

The battlefield has not slain him."

But father Bel could not help him.

[In his sorrow, Gilgamesh addresses himself then to the Moon-god, saying:]

"Father Sin, the sting of a fly has cast me down upon the ground;

Insects have brought me low to the ground.

Enkidu [has sunk down] to the shades;

Pestilence has not snatched him away, etc.

The lurking demon of Nergal, the merciless [has not snatched him away]."

[But Sin also could not do anything for Gilgamesh, nor could Ea, to whom he appealed with the same lament. But Ea besought Nergal, the god of the dead, the "hero and lord" (saying):]

"Break open the chamber of the grave [and open the ground],

that the spirit of Enkidu, like a wind,

may rise out of the ground."

When Nergal, the hero and lord, heard this prayer,

He broke open the chamber of the grave and opened the ground;

and caused the spirit of Enkidu to rise out of the ground, like a wind.

Col. IV begins with a dialogue between Gilgamesh and Enkidu; the former asking his friend to describe unto him the netherworld:

"Tell me, my friend, O tell me, my friend;

the appearance (?, looks) of the land, which thou hast seen, O tell me!"

But Enkidu replied:

"I can not tell thee, my friend, I can not tell thee.

If I would describe to thee the appearance of the land that I have seen,

[surely, Gilgamesh, thou wouldst?] sit down and weep."

[And Gilgamesh said unto him?]: "Then let me sit down and weep!

[Bitter and sad?] is all that formerly gladdened thy heart.

[All is there—i. e., in the netherworld?] like an old garment that the worm does eat.

What thou hast done [while in this life?], what formerly gladdened thy heart.

[All is gone?] is cloaked in dust.'

The rest of Col. IV and the whole of Col. V are lost. Col. VI closes the whole epic, with Enkidu's description of the joys awaiting the hero slain in battle and having received due burial; and bewailing the unhappy, miserable lot of the man to whom are denied the last burial rites; the important lesson for all readers of the poem being, "Take good care of your dead." He is properly cared for who--

rests on a soft couch, and drinks pure water; the hero slain in battle--

Thou and I have often seen such an one—

His father and mother support his head,

and his wife [kneels] at his side.

Yea! the spirit of such a man is at rest.

But the man whose corpse remains [unburied] upon the field--

Thou and I have often seen such an one—

His spirit does not find rest in the earth (i. e., Hades).

The man whose spirit has no one who cares for it--

Thou and I have often seen such an one—

consumes the dregs of the bowl, the broken remnants of food,

that are cast into the street.

Then follows the colophon of Tablet XII, and of the whole poem, which thus has come to an end.

According to Professor Haupt ("Contributions to Assyriology," vol. i, pp. 318, 319), plates 16-19 of his edition of the Nimrod-epic belong to Tablet XII; Dr. Jeremias, on the other hand, is inclined to believe that these fragments formed part of another recension of the same poem. The fact that there were several recensions of the account of the deluge goes far to strengthen the contention of Dr. Jeremias. The fragments, printed on plates 16-19, are portions of Cols. III and IV of (?) tablet. The mention of the hunter (see above, p. 327); of the Shamhat; the address, "my friend," show that Enkidu is the speaker. In Col. III he curses the Shamhat, who with the assistance of the crafty hunter had "brought a curse upon him." He hopes that "she will be imprisoned in the great prison," curses "her charms," "her sisters," and "her maidens." Col. IV (pp. 17 and 19 of Haupt's edition) states the reason why Enkidu curses the Shamhat (or perhaps Ishtar directly). Enkidu has gone down into the netherworld, and he tells his friend, who with the help of witchcraft has succeeded in bringing him up again, what he has seen there:

"* * * has brought me back

* * * like as the bird of darkness.

I have descended?] to the house of darkness, the dwelling of the goddess Irkalla;

to the house, whence he that enters goes out no more;

to the road, whose way turns not back;

to the house, whose inhabitants are deprived of light;

to the place where dust is their sustenance, their food clay.

They are clothed, like a bird, with feathered raiment (?).

Light they see not, they sit in darkness.

In] the house, my friend, which I have entered,

in that house] crowns are cast down on the ground,

and there live those who had worn crowns, who in days of old had ruled countries;

to whom Anu and Belit had given roasted meat to eat.

Now, cold meals are prepared, and water from leather bottles is poured out for them.

In the house, my friend, which I have entered,

there dwell also priests and ministers;

There dwell soothsayers and enchanters;

there dwell the temple-anointers of the great gods.

There dwells Etana, and there dwells Ner;

There dwells also the queen of the earth (i. e., of Hades), the goddess Ereshkigal (i. e., Allatu).

[There dwells?] the scribe of the earth, bowed down before her.

* * * and reads before her,

and Ereshkigal lifted up] her head and saw me."

THE END